CONFESSIONS
of a
MUNICIPAL BOND SALESMAN

CONFESSIONS
— *of a* —
MUNICIPAL BOND
SALESMAN

JIM LEBENTHAL
WITH BERNICE KANNER

WILEY
John Wiley & Sons, Inc.

Published by John Wiley & Sons, Inc., Hoboken, New Jersey.
Published simultaneously in Canada.

For general information on our other products and services or for technical
support, please contact our Customer Care Department within the United
States at (800) 762-2974, outside the United States at (317) 572-3993 or fax
(317) 572-4002.

Wiley also publishes its books in a variety of electronic formats. Some content
that appears in print may not be available in electronic books. For more
information about Wiley products, visit our web site at www.wiley.com.

Library of Congress Cataloging-in-Publication Data:

Lebenthal, Jim, 1928–
  Confessions of a municipal bond salesman / Jim Lebenthal with
Bernice Kanner.
      p.   cm.
  ISBN-13 978-0-471-77174-6 (cloth)
  ISBN-10 0-471-77174-0 (cloth)
  1. Lebenthal, Jim, 1928- 2. Municipal bonds—United States.
3. Brokers—United States—Biography. I. Kanner, Bernice. II.
Title.
  HG4952.L43L43   2006
  332.6'2092—dc22
                                      2005034342

Printed in the United States of America.

10 9 8 7 6 5 4 3 2 1

To Maria Canosa, Ron Holland, Jackie, and our three kids.

Thank you, Maria, for taking care of Jackie, for giving her a life, and providing me with the peace of mind to go off and write a very entertaining book.

Thank you, Ron, for 15 years of laugh therapy, while learning how to write spoken English at the master's knee.

Without the two of you, I would have bobbed and wobbled through these pages like the Scarecrow in the *Wizard of Oz.* Instead, here is good, sound horse sense about business, and not just straw coming out of a stuffed shirt.

And Jackie, darling, to you and our three excellent children, Claudia, Alexandra, and Jimmy to whom I have tried to be like, well, a father.

Foreword

If you know Jim Lebenthal—if you've been a target for his ads and sensed his exuberance for all things—then you really need this book. *Confessions of a Municipal Bond Salesman* fills in all those gaps in what you know. It connects the dots between an orthodox prep school/Ivy League education, a Hollywood fling, and the long years taking the obscure family business of trading dull municipal bonds from a by-way of Wall Street to an icon of New York City.

Maybe, just maybe, you don't know who Jim Lebenthal is: you never bought a "muni" bond, you don't live in New York, or care about movie land in the 1950s—you are not even a member of Princeton's class of 1949. Then you have a special treat in store. Jim Lebenthal is, always has been, and will always be, a salesman. There are as many insights in this book about the do's and don'ts of salesmanship as in any of the "business" books listed by Amazon or resting on the shelves of Barnes & Noble. The difference is that the Lebenthal lessons come with irrepressible good humor and sense of a larger purpose, quite a combination.

It all makes a great, honest, and mostly reassuring story. Jim Lebenthal could have found—indeed for a while did find—a career in the fast lane. *Life* magazine's man in Hollywood, an imaginative documentary, had him meeting the Marilyn Monroes and other glamour girls of our youth and put him well on his way. But somehow, family tradition, and family responsibilities, tugged hard. So back to New York, back to the family business, back to understudying Sayra—the family matriarch, mistress of Lebenthal & Company, and a trusted and trusting model of dedication to clients.

But it was the son who made the Lebenthal name a part of New York. There he was, live in your face every week in the *New York Times* or on TV: Jim Lebenthal 100 feet underground in the new water tunnel; Jim Lebenthal popping out of a manhole; Jim Lebenthal standing before the Verrazano Bridge as if he owned it, all equating the bonds he sold to the City's bridges, to its water supply, and yes, to its sewers and subways.

"Love my sewers, love my bonds!" Brilliant advertising to be sure, but it carried a serious message as well. The ability of states and localities to issue tax-exempt bonds is a key to building the infrastructure of New York, and of every city and town across America. It's a privilege that must not be abused.

And then a parable of American finance winds through the narrative. There is the family business nurtured with pride through three generations, with the circle completed with a new matriarch by way of Jim's daughter Alexandra. In the end, like so many others, the family enterprise couldn't withstand the logic of Wall Street—the urge to merge, to diversify, to capitalize on success. And so, for now, the Lebenthal name has been lost, gone from the bond business, but not from this memoir of a man.

Jim Lebenthal is as lively as ever, camera in hand capturing the splendor and the squalor, the diversity and the energy of the city he loves. Somehow even a cynical old timer like me can't resist his joie de vivre.

What better recommendation can I give?

PAUL VOLCKER
Former Chairman
of the Board of Governors
of the Federal Reserve System

Contents

CONFESSIONS
of a
MUNICIPAL BOND
SALESMAN

1

This Is Me

See It. Make It Art.

I owe a beer to two Princeton seniors for what I call a "Lebenthal, Aha! Moment," one of those epiphanies between shouting "Eureka!" and the quiet dawning of a truth.

First, you should know that I am one of those guys who puts the bite on classmates to give money year after year to Princeton, even 50 years after graduation. To help me work the feeling of today's Princetonians into one of my dunning letters, the university set up a lunch for me with five of the best and the brightest graduating seniors to find out what they planned to be doing one day with their Princeton educations. I hate to admit it, but I got more out of that luncheon than "Old Nassau" did, just from one student picking on a remark that popped out of another's mouth: "I want to understand the world, and then I want to teach what's possible," said Laura Shackelton, Oxford

1

bound, molecular biologist to be. She labeled her life pursuit, "Cognition and Articulation."

Eyes at the table lit up, "Me too!" said Theater Major Chris Wendell, a Jimmy Stewart look-alike, drawl and all. "Except I want to transform my grasp of things into an art form, like theater, so that I can make audiences see and hear the world through my eyes."

Whoa! In a flash of insight, I thought, That's just what I've been doing all my working life, including in my family's municipal bond business: seeing and then turning what I see into art for others to see what I see, and say, "Aha! I get it, too."

Thank you, Laura and Chris for opening my eyes. I want you to remember something as long as you live. I owe you both a beer.

Next Slide, Please!

I am a municipal bond salesman—with this twist.

I am also an incorrigible showman.

"Don't tell me, show me!" insisted the boss at my first job, for *Life* magazine. So, when I joined the Lebenthal family bond business (after 12 kaleidoscopic years following graduation, as a reporter, moviemaker, TV producer, and adman), believe me. I showed them all right. And how! With bold advertising in mass media.

I got up there on TV and, spreading my open arms across a sea of bearer bonds displayed on my desk, infused them with life. "I'm Jim Lebenthal," I proclaimed. "Municipal bonds are my babies!"

Over the years, I have turned those two words, *municipal bonds,* into "Lebenthal's Babies," "Lebenthal's Workhorse," "Lebenthal's Cash Cow." And I didn't stop the show until "Municipal Bonds Are My Babies" became household words, and "Lebenthal" became the most powerful sales tool there will ever be in commerce: a brand. Man for man, pound for pound, the name Lebenthal probably sold more municipal bonds than any other firm you can name on Wall Street. And when I think about all the times strangers have stopped me on the street and asked, "How are your babies, Jim?" Well . . . let me say that I have had more than my 15 minutes of fame.

I may walk the walk and dress the dress of a bond salesman. But in Dad's silent home movies, there are clear signs of other than just the municipal bond salesman to come. Entirely on my own—without being directed or told to move, act, or do something for the camera—I stuff a whole frankfurter into my mouth, somersault down a hill, wrap my leg around my neck, twist myself into a pretzel, stand on my head, canter my horse (no hands), jump off the garden furniture, swim on the grass, and squirm out of a hug from Mother.

Becoming that incorrigible showman, who one day would turn municipal bonds (and for that matter whatever I touched) into lively, graphic images, goes way back to when I was 7 years old, and a green truck from Railway Express pulled up to the door with a birthday package from my Aunt Dorothy.

Breathlessly, I unwrapped it and looked inside. Wow! A whole carton of my favorite food. How did Aunt Dorothy know I loved shredded coconut? I grabbed a handful and stuffed it in my mouth. Ugh! Shredded paper! But hidden in all that packing material was a Kodak Box Brownie. And that primitive camera would train my eye to look for the unexpected in the ordinary and find unexpected life in whatever exists, anywhere.

Just take what happened out West on Route 66, almost 50 years ago, when an unexpected something jumped in front of my car. I jammed on the brakes. In that tire screech, I realized: A tumbleweed blowing across the highway had fooled me into thinking it was alive. Instantly, I knew what I had to do: "You rascal you! I'm going to make a movie about an imp getting his comeuppance, starring you, Mister Tumbleweed. And together, you know what? We're going to win an Academy Award."

Well, I did make the movie; it was a short subject I called *"T Is for Tumbleweed."* And, by god, it actually did get nominated for an Oscar. *"Nominated."* That is when, on that magic Hollywood night, they say, "The envelope please . . . and the winner is . . ." But sitting there in my nominee's seat at the Oscars, all that I heard was "the envelope please . . . and the loser is . . . Jim Lebenthal!"

How long would it take me to get over not winning that statuette? A year . . . maybe even a lifetime. But something the projectionist said at the premiere of *Tumbleweed* will forever ring in my ears: "Lebenthal, when I watched that tumbleweed come to life up there on the screen," he said, handing me back my print, "I said to myself 'This guy could do a sequel with a leaf.'" He never knew how close he came. I did do a sequel. Only instead of a leaf, I starred something even drier. Over the next 40 years, I did for my tax-free municipal bonds what I had done for tumble-weeds. I gave them a face and personality and an exciting life of their own.

So where's the action and excitement in a municipal bond? I mean a tumbleweed at least tumbles. But a bond! You don't even get a crinkly engraved certificate. Nowadays, bonds come only in "Book Entry" form, a mere electronic blip on a giant computer. If New York City needs $1 billion for a new water tunnel, the City borrows it from firms like mine. Blip! We turn around and lay off that billion dollar loan: $10,000 here, $25,000 there—Blip! Blip!—to someone, maybe someone just like you. Your name goes into the computer. Then every 6 months, you get a credit at a firm like ours for your interest—Blip!—and at the end, when the bond matures, another credit—Blip!—when you get back the bond's full face value.

Where's the drama in that? Where's the theater?

No plot for an Oscar-winning movie there. Right?

But that is just the challenge I live for. I turn the impossible into pictures. If there is a concrete graphic image to be found in earning a tax-free income that is all yours to keep every time you receive an interest payment, my job is to find it. Because I am a camera. I really am. It doesn't matter whether I have a camera in my hands. I think in pictures. I feel in pictures. I talk in pictures, just as though I had one of those crickets in my hand for changing slides and a Kodak Carousel Projector in my brain. Now, if you will douse the lights, I will show you exactly what I mean: a virtual slide show of me growing up. "First slide, please! Click!"

You are looking at me, rolling around on the floor in second grade. I am doubled up with laughter because Miss Barry has just said the funniest word I ever heard, "I'll have none of your monkeyshines, Jimmy Lebenthal." Click! Next slide, please!

This is Mother under the hair dryer at the beauty parlor. I'm in fourth grade. I have just come running in after school to plead with her, "I don't want to play football. Please Mother, write me a note and get me out of football." But with all that hair dryer noise, she doesn't hear a word I am saying. Next slide, please! Click!

Me on the corner of Fifth Avenue and Fifty-third Street, stunned. I have just been slapped by a cop for making a wisecrack about his chewing out a driver. You can't see because I'm wearing a blue serge suit. But I just wet my pants. Click!

Close your eyes, here I am posing nude at Andover for some questionable "scientific" study in the 1940s and 1950s on the connection between physiology and intelligence. (Even Jackie Bouvier had to take it all off and pose.) Click!

This is Colonel Horace Poynter, the scariest teacher at Andover, who gave me a barely passing "60" in Latin but actually added an "A" for effort. That A meant superlative, more than can be humanly expected. Click!

An irrepressible me in blackface impersonating Jolson singing "Mammy." Click!

That proud 4-year old charioteer on the back of the little girl's tricycle is me, letting my friend Judy pedal us down Maple Avenue in Red Bank, New Jersey. Click!

In second grade the love of my life was Jean, the Shirley Temple of P.S. 75. Her "Good Ship Lollipop" and "Who's Afraid of the Big Bad Wolf?" were to die for. Click!

And this is Allegra! Shy, glamorous Allegra Fuller, whose slipping out of class early on Fridays for her figure skating or ballet lesson just heightened her allure of the un-attainable. Click!

The day the temperature almost hit a hundred at the 1939 World's Fair. Talk about unattainable. Unattainable to whom? That's my pal, Buddy Oppenheimer, arm in arm with guess who? Allegra! And me with rivulets of molten Sta-Comb running down my face, stuck with Allegra's mother. Buddy and I have just dragged Allegra and her mother to "The Crystal Lassies," a skin show in the Amuse-ment Section. And Mrs. Fuller has just dragged us right out of there. Sixty-seven years later, I remember exactly what she said, "Oh, boys! This isn't for us." I say, God bless those thwarted puppy loves of mine. Just intimations of the ro-mantic soul that one day would infuse whatever I touch with unbankerly passion. Lights on, please!

"Has Anybody Seen Jim?"

I came noisily into this world as "baby boy" Lebenthal on June 22, 1928 (My full name, James Avram, followed in an-other day or so). Mom and Dad already had a 3-year-old company and a 15-month-old baby girl Eleanor on their hands. Mine was an unspectacular childhood filled with spectacular delights. I could turn any treat, say a trip to

Radio City Music Hall, into the thrill of a lifetime just like that (e.g., by dashing pell-mell at intermission to the very front of the house—first row, far right—to gawk at the snare drummer in the orchestra pit). At home, my idea of a joke was to hide behind the sofa, with a microphone in hand hooked up to the radio, announcing, "We interrupt this broadcast to bring you a special news bulletin." And Mother and Dad played along by wondering out loud, "Isn't that awful news? And by the way, has anybody seen Jim?" It was an uneventful childhood until Dad got sick and, for a long time, a quiet fell over our house.

Starting in the 1940s, Dad suffered a series of debilitating strokes that slowed him and diminished him until he died in 1951. Mom kept her sanity by keeping Lebenthal & Company purring, while I sowed my oats in Hollywood and on Madison Avenue, and pursued a kaleidoscopic interlude first with tumbleweeds and then with my otters, Flash and Missy, the stars of my movie for Walt Disney, *Flash, The Teenage Otter.*

I was 25 and a bachelor when I covered the movies and the Hollywood stars for *Life* magazine. I remember one candidate for the cover of the magazine, an outspoken 17-year-old from Britain. The photographer asked her for more expression. "Be animated! Talk to Jim!" And did she talk! She said, "I think for a boy your age to have a figure like the shape of a pear is perfectly disgusting." And who was that sassy starlet? A gorgeous, fresh Joan Collins, long, long before *Dynasty.*

As it happens, I weighed 187 at the time and was in perfect shape (for a pear). Nevertheless, I went on a drastic diet and workout regimen. A few months later, the lean, lanky figure of a Greek god stood in the doorway of Joan's dressing room. "Okay!" I said, "How do I look now?" "A bit better, Darling, but move away," she said, "You're still blocking my light."

I remember the time Grace Kelly and I rode to the Oscars in her limo. . . . I remember getting a "yok" out of the great silent moviemaker Mack Sennett. It was when he and I coauthored a special Keystone Kops comedy to run as a picture story in *Life*. (Sennett, a comic genius, never laughed—if something struck him as funny, he grudgingly conceded, "That's a yok. That's a yok.") I dealt with the Hollywood rebels who loved holding the press corps in icy contempt. I melted a truculent James Dean and got him to open up his soul for *Life*. And I personally arranged for Rock Hudson to have a few more years in the closet, so he could appear on the cover of *Life* without corrupting the morals of our readers. How did I do it? By dispatching Rock off to Mexico for a convenient marriage to his agent's secretary, Phyllis Gates.

What a mindless, rollicking, fun-filled, party life I had at *Life!* Can you believe anyone would pull the plug on such a glamorous life? I certainly can't . . . but I did.

I was 35 when I answered the siren call.

Back in New York, my mother, Sayra Lebenthal, was hard at work running Lebenthal & Company, the Oldest House in America Specializing in Odd Lot Municipal Bonds.

Mom was awfully smart about pressure. Throughout my travels (and her travails), she never pleaded, never needled, never twisted my arm to stop the nonsense and come into the family bond business. Because she didn't have to.

9

She knew that just knowing Lebenthal & Company was there would eventually wear me down.

It happened all by itself one night at a Hollywood celebrity party. Right while I was delivering a stream of one-liners that had the circle around me laughing and begging me, "Please, Jim, go on the stage! See Lew Wasserman! Get MCA to handle you." Enticing, but I had second thoughts.

After a decade of having far too much fun working for Henry Luce, Walt Disney, and David Ogilvy, I started to grill myself: What am I doing out here? Why am I making other companies famous, when I could be building an empire for Lebenthal and putting my family's name on every tongue?

At last I made the call Mother was waiting for. "Mom, I've decided to come to work at Lebenthal & Company."

Silence.

"Mother!" More silence.

"Mom?"

"At last," she said, "you finally got all that foolishness out of your system. It's about time!" Click, over, and out!

I never did get "all that foolishness" out of my system. I never did lose my passion for seeing the ordinary and turning it into art. And it's a damned good thing. Because, seeing and showing demystified what was the most un-understandable investment in America (until I came along), opened the window, and let the fresh air in. The kind of foolishness that let me turn municipal bonds into My Babies made a musty Wall Street product crackle with vitality. And for Lebenthal, well frankly, that foolishness turned into money in the bank.

10

Now, in my senior years, I'm looking back to find out what worked for me, as I built my family's modest odd-lot bond house into the best-known municipal bond firm in America and then passed it along to my smarter-than-I daughter—Alexandra. Much of the time what I did was fly by the seat of my ants-in-the-pants pants. Only by applying the brake pedal of my left brain to my intuitive revved up right brain, am I able to articulate the unhesitant steps that led me from Point A to Point Q.

Like so many authorities who imperiously proclaim that their belief is their authority and assertion is their proof, I seldom could explain the logic of what I did at the time. I just knew in my heart of hearts that I was right— mistakes, gaffes, goofs, and all. Now from the perspective of age, here is what *I think* I was thinking.

By following along, you, too, can become the next great municipal bond salesperson. Or anything else for that matter. Listen to how I did it, then relate it to your own life, and chances are you will find the courage to listen to your own heart and inner voice. Maybe there is some pixie dust here for you.

LEBENTHAL TO GO

Want to be an artist?
"If you see something,
say something," or reverse it.
When you say something,
make people see something.

Happy at work?
Just ask yourself, if it didn't pay,
would I still want this job
for a hobby?

There's nothing wrong with
switching jobs. Just make sure
you don't quit the old one
without a success under your belt.

If at first you don't succeed, try,
try again. (Of course it helps to
have a family business to fall
back on, like, guess who?)

2

Songs My Mother Taught Me

What Kind of Boss Was My Mother? What Kind of Mother Was My Boss?

At the beginning I sat across from Sayra Lebenthal, the founding mother, at the opposite side of her half-moon desk. I cut my teeth making phone calls to prospects who had once answered a Lebenthal ad but had never stepped up to the plate and bought themselves a bond. While I groped my brain for the right words to say, my mother, all 4 feet 11 inches of her, perched at the ready in her swivel chair. Her feet didn't quite reach the floor but were propped on a stool beneath her. She listened in on a telephone extension tapped into mine, just waiting to mouth to me what I should say. Pithy gems like, "One basis point is one $\frac{1}{100}$th of 1 percent. . . . Yield up means price down. . . . You buy municipal bonds for income, not to make money from market moves. . . . Oh, no, no, no, inflation is bad for bonds." Although in my thinking I was a fledgling learning from the mama bird how to fly and sing for my supper, listen to her as this dynamo wielded her expertise and common sense on her own hesitant customers:

> By all means, discuss it with your husband, Thelma. But I have a feeling you're the one who wears the pants in the family.
>
> You remember the last time you and Arthur bought a two-year bond? And what happened in two years when it matured and you had to reinvest? Interest rates came down, and you were out in the cold.
>
> The extra cost of a premium comes right back to you in the coupon along with the interest. You're afraid it's that much less you'll be leaving heirs? Heirs should be grateful for small favors, dear!
>
> Faint heart never won fair lady, Carl.

Eavesdropping on mother in action was pure entertainment. Here's a sample:

> "Good morning, Walter. How are you? This is Sayra Lebenthal." [She is practically yelling into the receiver because she knows Walter, a client for more than 20 years, is a bit hard of hearing these days.]

14

"Do you have any money? . . . No? Forget that I even called." Next a call to a wealthy Park Avenue dentist who says he will have to get back to her. ["He's between cavities," Mrs. L explains.] Then she dials a prominent Manhattan developer, the son of a late Lebenthal bond buyer, who will be known here as Mr. Greenbaum. "I'm sitting here with some lovely, lovely New York State general obligation bonds, fully registered." She recites a lengthy description of the bond's details. But young Mr. Greenbaum questions whether he might get a better yield by waiting awhile. Mrs. L, not wanting this one to get away, turns on the voice of experience. "I've only sat here for 60 years or more, Mr. Greenbaum. So let me give you a little advice. You cannot beat a market. Who knows what tomorrow or the next day will bring? Nobody can tell you what'll happen in 15 minutes. Somebody can sneeze their heads off in Washington, and the whole market can go to hell." Another few minutes of the lecture, Mr. Greenbaum manages to get in a single word, "Yes," and $60,000 worth of New York State bonds have been sold. (Roger Cohn, "Mama Don't Preach," *Manhattan, Inc.*, July 1988)

Mother could sell municipal bonds as easily as if they were jelly beans because she was a bond buyer herself. She bought when she had the money and she never tried to get in at the bottom or out at the top. When a bond came due and paid off, she just rolled over the proceeds and reinvested in more bonds at the going rate of interest. Her written philosophy was the first thing visitors saw as they walked into Lebenthal & Company. There, in a picture frame painted with pretty flowers, was this open letter from Mother anyone could read, dated August 24, 1973:

I don't mind the normal risks of business. Prices going up. Prices going down. But I do mind the abnormal risks. Dishonesty. A salesman saying something that isn't true. Getting involved in a client's dishonesty. After 47 years in business—through the Great Depressions, three wars, and six recessions—sure I'm concerned when the market goes up or down, but that's normal risk of doing business. When I look back at the 1920s, the 1930s, the 1940s, or just last week, who are my happiest clients? The ones who feel the way I do and don't try to outsmart the market. And when I look forward to the next 53 years (and Lebenthal's 100th year in business), they'll still be happier than the experts who call me all worried, and tell me that the papers say interest rates are going up.
[Signed] Sayra Lebenthal

When I finally joined the family bond business in 1962, Mother was my boss and teacher. The "Motherisms" I absorbed from her would one day become verities I'd fight for and defend. Like these: Municipal bonds are safe. Mu-

16

nicipal bonds are tax-free. Municipal bonds are marketable. If you hold to maturity, you will get back full face value. But if you have to sell before maturity, go ahead. Sell! Just make sure you buy bonds other firms will bid on, and not just the one outfit that sold them to you. In my Mother's book, any municipal bond worth its salt had to provide safety of principal, assuredness of interest, and marketability. Period, over, and out!

Instead of hiding that a 35-year-old man was learning the bond business, not from the Harvard Business School, not from Wall Street, but from his mother, I ran an ad that told the charming truth. The headline was "Everything My Mother Taught Me about Municipal Bonds—And a Few Things She Didn't." And it showed me at the age of three sitting on Mother's lap. I ran the ad at a time when any bond house was happy with a cost per lead of $75. "Everything My Mother Taught Me . . ." produced leads costing $3 each. But we had to stop running it. It seemed the brokers were mostly answering phone calls from people who thought I was adorable.

Scoldings as Expression of Endearment

I keep the first letter to Mother I ever wrote framed on the credenza in my office. It is undated, but considering that the letterhead is from a camp I went to in 1933, I guess I wrote it when I was five. The block letters go uphill and down. The letter is unsigned, but my Neanderthal hand-writing is unmistakable:

> Dear Mother,
> Please Mother will you get me a cow boy suit. If you don't I will be very mad.

Another "Dear Mother" letter in a file dated 1942, written from Andover, continues in the same snotty tone:

> Before I forget to tell you I have a few requests. The first is that when I ask for something please send it or tell me why. I have a very good reason for this. All my stockings have holes in them. By the way, what president was it whose son died from a blister on the heel?

Mother deserved better from me, but even so she was pretty slow about giving in to the brat she would later indulge and dote on. That's why she gets an A for spoiling me slowly and being awfully good company. She read A. A. Milne to my sister Eleanor and me. When we yelled, "Ready!" she would come kiss us goodnight. She accompanied me on the piano while I tortured my violin. She was full of love and support. But not so fast, not so fast. She was no pushover. Mother did not ever just hand out blanket approval. Permission was always tinctured with admonition (just so she could be on record if anything went wrong). And in case the Fates were listening, she gave weight to every syllable: "Have you thought it over very carefully?" "Do you know whereof you speak?" "Have you discussed it with your lawyer?"

As a courtesy to Lebenthal's major stockholder, I had to pass things by Mother. This included the firm's intention to underwrite a closed-end fund of municipal bonds whose shares would be traded on the New York Stock Exchange (NYSE), for which I had concocted the unique selling proposition: "Triple-Tax-Free Income from a Common Stock." Common stock! Stock exchange! Anathema! I might as well have asked Mohammed to eat a pork chop. As a grown man, having to ask my mother's permission to go into a bond deal made me feel like a teenager asking Dad for the family car. First comes the lecture, "If you drive, don't drink. If you drink, don't drive." Only then come the keys. Whenever I presented ads for her approval, which she would invariably grant, as she did for "Triple-Tax-Free Income from a Common Stock," her eagle eye always found the elusive typo, and she would taunt me: "If you're going to run this ad, you'd better learn how to spell."

Just as Mother could temper her "yes" with a "but," she could also turn scolding one of her clients into an expression of endearment. "I don't mean to be cranky, Carl, but you've got to do the arithmetic, dear!" She once scolded a village clerk who had gone fishing: "I don't care if it was your day off. My July interest check came late and you're in technical default, dear!" Her lilting "dear" took out all the sting. Well, almost.

My mother could be as just and wise as Mickey Rooney's father, Judge Hardy, in the *Andy Hardy* movies.

When I was growing up, I had a little bout with indecent exposure. Eleanor caught me unzipped with the neighbor's daughter, and for a year of "I'll tell Mother . . ." threats, she had me in her power. When one day she finally did tell all, I pulled an act of stunned disbelief. I faked a dead faint, keeled over, and landed flat on my back. Mother barely acknowledged my misdeed. "Anything born of love is beautiful," she tut-tutted, and instead of turning her wrath on me, she scolded Eleanor for practicing blackmail, dear.

In what I came to call the "Sibling Wars" at Lebenthal, Eleanor and I fought over a mother's love and "equality." (Equality of pay, power, and, for all I know, a mother's hugs and kisses.) Eleanor was vice president in charge of daily operations and ran the back office like Master and Commander. At year end, the National Association of Securities Dealers (NASD) allowed securities firms 20 days leeway into January to close the books. Eleanor had it done by the stroke of midnight New Year's Eve and took her crew to the Rainbow Room for a midnight snack.

This Gloria Vanderbilt look-alike collected paper clips in the pocket of her smock. She saved used staples in a paper cup and rubber bands in a ball. She was the poster girl for Consumer Action Now (CAN). She condemned my painful writing block, not for the hours of my life wasted searching for the perfect word, but for the wasted paper in those crumpled balls on the floor.

I give credit to Mother for letting bullets bounce off her chest in the crossfire between Eleanor and me, and for laying down the law. Eleanor and I should accept her terms of employment—equality be damned—or else. What was the "or else?" We would just have to wait to discover that . . . at the reading of her will.

Age? Huh! It neither slowed Mother down nor mellowed her. She had been raised in Keyport, New Jersey, by a Russian immigrant father, Joseph Fischer, a widower who owned a local burlap-bag business and who retired in his 70s, too early, and thereafter withered rapidly and died. Mother learned her lesson well. As she approached her 90th birthday, she refused to think about retiring and railed against anyone suggesting it. She said she wanted to work until she had to be carried out because she didn't know how to play golf and she hated the idea of squandering a day in the mall shopping. Her one concession to turning 90: She started taking a cab to work instead of the subway. The little lady would engineer a seat in rush hour by instructing passengers to move a little over there, and angle a little over there. Then she would seat herself majestically, open up her Blue List (a daily listing of current intradealer bond offerings) and stretch it wide, oblivious of her seatmates, studying it for bargains.

It took years, but gradually, and ever so cautiously, she relinquished control of her firm. But not before Alexandra, her granddaughter and assistant at the time, went with me to Dr. Aaron Stern, psychiatrist to the elderly, to find out how to deal with "Paranoia of the 90-Year-Old in the Workplace." As Nana's sight, hearing, and speed were fading, she was darned if anyone was going to pull a fast one on her. She was getting increasingly touchy, losing her train of thought and blaming it on others. But she still held the reins as treasurer, senior salesperson, and majority stockholder with veto power over major decisions. "Slow down, speak up, explain things as often as it takes," Dr. Stern advised. "Understand what it must be like when the world starts passing you by and it's still your money on the line." Lo and behold, the doctor's good advice worked and stuck with Alexandra and me. We got Nana to sign her tax return, do a little estate planning, and let Eleanor pay her bills. And I notice Alexandra has slowed down with me and explains things to me, as often as it takes.

Mother bought municipal bonds with high coupon rates at big, fat premiums for her old age. "Old age" had always summoned up pictures of the sunset and Anne Hathaway's cottage—not of the wheezing respirators and hospital beds that would draw down her savings as her light faded. And not of the nurses who sat in the back row at Campbell's Funeral Chapel. The nurses saw more of mother than any of us did in those final years. But Mother would have been the first to say, "If you're going to sell your bonds, at least have something to show for it. Wear it in good health, dear."

And here I was, with power of attorney, indeed selling her bonds and dipping into capital to pay for her long-term care in her final three years. Irreverent as it might sound, the obvious fact occurred to me: "If Mother lives to 101, she and her last municipal bond will be redeemed on the same day." It's sad to think that at one time for a few thousand dollars a year, she could have bought an insurance policy that would have paid for the best in care and avoided destroying a portfolio she took years to build up. Her heirs might still be clipping the coupons on Mother's Patchogue 9s. And then, I hear a voice from the grave repeating her mantra, "Heirs should be grateful for small favors, dear."

How to Hurt a Guy

A mystery. Why would anyone ever dare call me a "mama's boy"?

Yes, I loved my mother. I felt awful when I jumped on the runners of a rocking chair where I thought she was sitting and, when I pulled it all the way back, stared into the shocked face of someone else's mother. In school plays, I always looked out to see if she was in the audience. I quit a great job at 35 and learned a new one at her knee. But that doesn't make me a mama's boy. Just because I needed love and attention? Had to do things my way? And my mother went along and indulged me? If giving in to my irrepressible urges and passions, listening to my pleas to turn Americans into savers and those savers into buyers of municipal bonds, and encouraging my desire to make something out of Lebenthal mean I was a spoiled, rotten mama's boy, then I'll plead guilty every time.

I did have a dream about jumping off a cliff to escape an indefinable something and trying to slow the fall with an umbrella. Umbrella is my amusing word for umbilical cord. Um-brel-la. Um-bil-ical? It could have been a mama's boy dream about letting go (or not letting go). Because in the dream, I realized the umbrella would turn itself inside out and I would only be jumping to my death. So I didn't jump. I just resigned myself to giving in to whatever I was running away from. Could it have been Mother? Lebenthal & Company? Who knows? I did go to a shrink once (for writer's block). He said, "Look. We can explore the relationship with the sister . . . father dead at 50 . . . this business of your worshipping women from afar . . . the conflicted identity—Is he a writer? Is he a photographer?—and of course the relationship with the mother. But I'm afraid if we lift that rock, we're just going to find a can of worms."

Sayra Lebenthal, accepting an award as "Businesswoman of the Year," once said, "I'll know I've arrived when one of my children says, 'My mother said . . .' and then quotes me." And so, my mother, who died in 1994 at age 95, must feel she's "arrived." Because when I try to sell someone a bond, it isn't just a sales call. It's my mentor talking through me. When I hear myself talking to clients on the telephone, I can hear the tone of voice of Mother, more than compensating for her 4 feet 11 inches in height, wielding her personal power like the lady on the Old Dutch Cleanser can, beating the daylights out of dirt. Sometimes it's like I'm just mouthing her words:

Do you realize how much that's worth in your tax bracket? 10 percent! They used to put people in jail for usury like that.

I say it's not a contest to outlive your bonds. The only virtue in matching maturity with your life expectancy is to startle your mourners as they realize that both the Departed and his bonds were redeemed on the same day.

Darling, if you're Britney Spears, you have all the time in the world. But if you are someone near my age, you better put on your Nikes and just do it.

I have no problem with a bond that depends on the stability of society. To me, human nature is not a force that drives man to the brink lemming-like. Instead, it's the saving grace that pulls him back.

Edna! If you're going to worry about everything, put your money in a mattress, dear, and don't smoke in bed!

LEBENTHAL TO GO

You're never too old
to listen to your mother.
For all you know,
she could be right.

When "My Momma Done
Told Me" amounts to on-the-
job training, even the littlest
lessons like "Be on time!"
take on the rule of gospel.

Physician, heal thyself,
and broker buy thy own long-term
care insurance. If what you're selling is
good for the customer,
then why isn't it good
enough for you?

Inside every difficult customer
is a 90-year-old convinced he (or she)
is the lone person against the
tank in Tiananmen Square . . . and
you're the driver. Slow down,
come to a complete stop,
and put yourself in the other guy's shoes.

3

Selling

You Personally Could Pass Such a Test, Madam?

Staying close to your money—holding it to your chest, counting it, feeling it, touching it—is the most natural thing in the world. So imagine what a sophisticated, civilized act it is for *Homo sapiens* to go against the grain and rent his money out. As a middleman who is persuading you to invest, I openly admit that investing is against your animal nature. If we brokers always seem to be nagging, pushing, pulling, tugging, pressuring, squeezing, leaning on you, it is because of this equation: There you are, doing what comes naturally—sitting on your cash—and here we are, asking you to get off your assets and "give us your money!"

There should be a prize for "Client of the Week." The winner would be Goldie Barr! Goldie is a retired bookkeeper who appeared in my office with a cheerful "here-I-am" smile and a $20,000 CD coming due. She said she wanted 4 percent triple-tax-free, and nothing that matures in the next century. She'd yield on yield, if I held a gun to her head. But not on maturity! Ten years max! I found her a $20,000 New York City general obligation, noncallable bond, maturing in a decade, and she promptly said, "Done! I didn't spend all that time on the subway to come down here for nothing."

Her display of decisiveness makes me wonder how come some people like Goldie can just walk in, ask what is good, buy it, and get it over with; whereas others approach buying municipal bonds as if they are playing "Dungeons & Dragons." They are haunted by the "Inflation Demon," "Bad Timing Demon," "Maturity Demon," "Liquidity Demon," and "Security Demon," that stalk them every step of the way:

> "I'm afraid Inflation could come back from the dead."
>
> "I'm scared I'll be paid off in dollars that are worth less."
>
> "I'm worried whatever I buy today will be cheaper tomorrow."
>
> "Suppose I have to sell, how much will I lose?"
>
> "The cities could go bust."
>
> "Tax exemption could be killed."
>
> And worst of all, "I won't be around when my bonds mature."

I can still hear the quaver in the voices of Mrs. Canon, Sid Siegel, and the Blocks. A full two decades earlier, I had settled them into 20-year commitments to bonds that would not be due until 2006. Well, what do you know? The year 2006 has come, and I am now replacing their old bonds with spanking new 20-year varietals. So you say 2026 seems so impossibly distant? I say no more so than the first *Star Wars,* Chernobyl, Granada, Mount Saint Helens, Watergate, Dave Garroway and his chimpanzee, J. Fred Muggs that, when you think about it, seem like they were only yesterday. Same thing with tomorrow and tomorrow. Time plays tricks as it morphs from present to future, and tomorrow is suddenly here before you know it. That's why there really ought to be a warning printed right the mirror of time: "Objects in the future are a lot closer than they appear." Fear not the year 2026 or for that matter 2036, just because you may not be here then.

After 80 years of hearing "I won't be around when my bonds mature," we Lebenthals have acquired this point of view about time. You should go into municipals for the good you get out of them every time you get your interest. It is not a contest to outlive your bonds. The only thing that happens at maturity is the contract is over and they send you, or your heirs, home with your money. Time is an investor's best friend.

Time may be a lousy beautician, but it is a great healer. Time smooths out the lumps. It turns the ups and downs that feel as if they will go on forever, into just another day on the way to San Jose. Time gives a newborn a chance to morph into a college sophomore, lets the pendulum swing the other way, and allows the grass and other green things to grow. Time, as the ageless Mick Jagger croons, "is on my side, yes it is."

And yet worrying about time, this business of weighing maturity against yield—whether to lend your money for 5 years and be grateful for, say, 3 percent (tax-free, of course) or lend it for 20 years and rake in 5 percent—is the toughest decision there is in picking and choosing a municipal bond. And nobody makes it harder—or tougher on me—than my client of long standing, who in respect for his privacy I will call by the handle I used when I would ask my assistant, "Get me the 'Tough Hombre' on the telephone."

Just listen to this for pouring hot chicken soup down the patient's throat:

LEBENTHAL: We just bought a bond I love that's right up your alley if you'll relinquish on this business of maturity. It is a 5.5 percent bond at a tremendous current return because it is selling at a tremendous discount: State of Florida 5½s of January 1, 2008. They're at a 9.40 percent yield to maturity, which works out to a dollar price of 63. In the meantime it is a current return for you in your lifetime now of 8.70 percent. Tax free.

TOUGH HOMBRE: That's a long time.

LEBENTHAL: A long time for what? That's a long time to have a cash cow that is constantly giving you the 8.70 percent. That's why you buy these bonds: for the 8.70 percent now. I'm not even discussing the yield to maturity of 9.40 percent. Let your grandchildren cash in the bond when it matures and enjoy the appreciation.

TOUGH HOMBRE: No, I think I'll pass.

LEBENTHAL: I'm mortified.

TOUGH HOMBRE: The maturity is just too long.

LEBENTHAL: That's because all you're hearing is the 2008 part. You're not hearing the 63 cents on the dollar. You're not hearing the 5.5 percent coupon rate, which on 63 cents gives you more return on a current yield basis than anything you're possibly going to find in your maturity range.

TOUGH HOMBRE: I won't go out any longer than 10 years.

LEBENTHAL: I have Oregons right in your range paying 6.75 percent—almost two full percentage points less than the Floridas. . . . Here are 10-year Clevelands at 6.87 percent. . . . You'd settle for 6.87 percent just to see your money back in 1993?

TOUGH HOMBRE: So many things can happen. You know, the dollar can go down. . . .

LEBENTHAL: When you say so many things can happen. I want you to be fair about it. So many things can happen including the dollar could go up, including inflation could stay at 4 percent, including all the good news. Why is it that when everybody says they're uncertain, they never include anything that could happen in their favor? Let the dollar go up, let the dollar go down, let all that stuff happen. Every day you hold this bond, it is approaching its face value. Par! So that if you had to sell it back to Lebenthal in five years at a price to give the next investor a 10.40 percent yield to maturity (because all the doom and gloom has happened), the price you'd get would still be more than you paid for it. And all the time that you held the Floridas, you would have been getting 8.70 percent. . . .

31

TOUGH HOMBRE: Mr. Lebenthal, did I ever tell you, you are a terrific salesman?

LEBENTHAL: I'm only a terrific salesman when you say, "I buy!"

TOUGH HOMBRE: Well, I just said it, didn't I?

LEBENTHAL: I'm selling you, $25,000, State of Florida General Obligation 5½s of January 1, 2008/noncallable, at a price to yield 9.40 percent to maturity which works out to a dollar price of approximately 63. With accrued interest, it will be just under $16,000. Somewhere in that neighborhood.

TOUGH HOMBRE: I buy!

LEBENTHAL: Good for you. You did the right thing. So let me say thank you very much and hang up before I kill the sale.

You can try to jolly the customer who says he won't be here in the year 2026 by asking to see his X-rays. Or slowly, calmly, logically explain the arithmetic to the client who hates to pay premiums. (Instead of getting the nine point premium back at the end, he gets it back right along as part of the interest being spun off by the coupon.) We munibond salespeople have to choose when to fight emotion with emotion or reason with reason.

Allen Funt, who created *Candid Camera,* was a good customer with a psychological hurdle. He once confided that when he was a boy he had a horse that would shy at mailboxes no matter what Allen did to calm that horse or hustle it past mailboxes. "Jim," he told me, "premium bonds are my mailboxes."

Allen urged me to stop beating my head against the wall and not offer him any bonds with premiums. I had another idea. The next time I called Allen, I asked to talk to his horse. Or to tell his horse, "I've got a mailbox he'll love." Funt got both the joke and the bond. Jocularity worked where reason had failed. It was a case of going into battle with a feather and winning by tickling Allen with the folly of his ways.

I remember one day when my great and good friend (and Princeton classmate), Paul Volcker, former chairman of the Federal Reserve Board was peppering me with questions about price and yield, security, and even the bond's tax-exempt status. "Paul," I said, "You remind me of the woman buying a chicken. First she lifts one leg, sniffs, puts it down . . . then the other leg, sniffs and puts it down . . . then a wing and sniffs. As she lifts the other wing, the butcher stops her, 'Tell me, Mrs. Nussbaum, could you personally pass such a test?'" Then I added, "Paul, you get three more questions. If I pass, you've got to buy the bonds, okay?"

"G'bye" sighed the genial chairman, "Send them in."

I joked with a woman I always called the "Vixen" (behind her back) because she was always sitting on her haunches, howling at the moon for something better to come along. I waxed too charming, too disarming, too funny, and too wonderful with her. She caved, bought my bond . . . and next day canceled. There is nothing worse than that in my business. It means the broker pushed too hard and had never really clinched the sale. It takes a heap of reselling to hold someone to a trade who wants out. I

happened to have a camera rolling when I held a trade together for another broker who had a classic problem: Her
client went home and told his wife what he had bought!
This is just my side of the telephone conversation:

LEBENTHAL: You're not the first person who's ever had to
go home and face the missus. I just wish you had
bought an even longer bond. If you bought your house
the way you're now telling me you should buy your
bonds, you'd be living in a Japanese hut made out of
shoji screen, and after one rain you'd be out in the
cold. A bond should last as long as your house. . . . Alright! Say you did need the money now and had to sell.
Your bonds have been up. They've been down. Right
now they're down. They'll be up again. But do you
know what I want you to do? I want you to thank God
you don't have to sell. Because for each day you don't
have to sell, you've living off the fat of the land. You're
getting the equivalent of 12.90 percent in your
bracket. . . . It's when you go home and all of a sudden
have to intellectualize what you did that you fall apart,
even when you impulsively did the right thing. . . . All
right, let her say something . . . Delia! Listen to me. Listen to me because you've got to keep peace in the family. Stop telling Harry he made a big stupid mistake.
Don't keep grinding that in, you're going to make
wreck of him. . . . Now Delia . . . Delia, Delia, Delia.
How can I get you to calm down? What's for supper
tonight? . . . Fish? At today's prices! What kind of

fish? . . . Then do that, relax and think what you're going to make for supper and stop rocking the boat. . . . I tell you he did the right thing. . . . Good, good, good. It's done. No more about it. . . . Now, I'm going to say goodbye. . . . Go have the fish.

Shut Up and Listen

To give the suspicious first-time investor the confidence to make the leap from banks to bonds, takes someone who is half teacher, half economist, half psychologist, and full-time listener. Let me share with you a session I had with one of our brokers. He was talking a lot, intent on showing how quick he was and not letting things sink in before coming up like thunder with a recommendation.

I pointed out that, for all his long hours on the telephone, fast talk was destroying his credibility. It denied him that rush of accomplishment from finally finding the bond that really fits a client. Our clients are looking for a kindred spirit who will match the right investment to their needs, treat them like family, and in fact be their brother's keeper.

Salespeople are not listening well if they don't learn enough about their customers to know what to recommend. Whatever recommendation they make without foundation will come off as slick. Fast talkers simply do not relate to people. And it is only the relationship that gives a salesperson a license to do the transaction. Relationships begin when someone talks and someone else listens. Being the listener virtually ensures a successful relationship.

I urged this new broker, for one week, not to sell on the first call—just to dial, listen to the client, and let it sink in. Then he would be able to call someone back with an offering that mirrored what he had learned. He needed to wait for the Eureka Moment. It would come.

Amazingly, the broker took my advice. He began to talk less and sell more. But alas for him, the fizz had gone out of the job. He missed the sound of his own voice.

I, too, quit Lebenthal & Company once. I loved the digging and probing, the listening and getting to know my fellow human beings, albeit human beings with money. But sculpting one individual at a time, not in clay, but in long-term/short-term, high coupon/low coupon, premium/discount bonds just wasn't enough. So I jumped ship to join Ogilvy & Mather Advertising as a creative supervisor for IBM's corporate advertising. Mother was philosophical about my departure: "It isn't that Jim hasn't found himself. He just doesn't know where to put it yet. He'll be back."

The Return of the "Talking Surgeon"

Sure enough, two years later there I was back again—wiser, worldlier, and *wordier*. I, the ex-explainer of IBM computers, now back at Lebenthal, was writing the company's weekly newsletters and educational materials. But I was still on the telephone dialing-for-dollars—and I was dumping out on my customer's head whatever I had just written that week about municipal bonds. I had a name for my routine of selling by telling everything I know: The Talking Surgeon. "I'm cutting through the epidermis and clamping back flaps of flesh and getting down now into real muscle. . . ." Spare me the gory details I would ask of the salesman we had at Lebenthal who also worshipped at the altar of full disclosure and talked too much.

This guy regarded every sales call as his big chance to show off his prodigious knowledge about his product. The only way he could tell he had given his prospect enough information was when the client finally gave up and scuttled away from the assault with a feeble "thanks but no thanks." The broker was honest, well meaning, and worth saving. I knew him well, for he was the son of the founder—me!

Working in a business that bore my family's name meant that, rather than show me the door, they decided to show me the way. They sent me to *Growth Skills,* one of those sales training outfits that analyze your preparedness to sell after a weekend of role playing and then demonstrate how to fix what's wrong. Their advice: Learn better how to balance giving and getting. Recognize the little ways in which people take advantage, at times without your even knowing it. They advised me to become a little more calculating, and balance my nice guy image with the "ability to convey indignation as well as to act cold or even a little threatening." Every so often, they advised, I should be the one "to show willingness to risk a break in the relationship."

37

Look into My Eyes,
and Buy My Bond

While I certainly didn't find that very useful, what *was* a fabulous result of that weekend was the consultant's advice not to dump out a thousand well-chosen words when clients asked why I wanted them to buy a bond. "Just say, because I want you to," he advised. "Use personal power instead of persuasion by explanation."

"Oh I get it," I replied. "I should say, 'Because I want you to!' and then go into my reasons."

"No!" my counselor exploded. "Just repeat, 'Because I want you to buy it.' That is your *only* explanation."

"Because I want you to buy it."

It took all my self-restraint to cut down on my song and dance, and sell by wielding "Personal Power" instead of trying to show off how much I knew. Of course, you still have to know your product. But like the armature inside a piece of sculpture giving the figure of the ballet dancer form and grace, product knowledge is not supposed to stick out and show. Soon enough, I learned Personal Power works, and was using its brute force on Sister Mary Virginia to get a very young Alexandra Lebenthal switched out of her scary Latin class at St. Hilda's & St. Hugh's, ruled by Sister with a hickory stick. And I used the same technique to sell $25,000 worth of an impossibly complicated bond issue to a bewildered client. "Here's the deal," I told him. "I can either describe how the Puerto Rico Government Development Bank is laying off a loan it made to the Health Authority so it can pay you 9 percent guaranteed by a Letter of Credit from the Credit Industrial Development Bank of Japan . . . or I can simply circle you for $25,000 of the bonds. What do you say?" He said, "Put me down for $25,000."

And Now the $1,845,000,000,000 Question

You could argue that the name Lebenthal alone might convince someone, "This guy knows his beans before he even opens his mouth." But even when I was writing those knowledgeable Lebenthal newsletters, I was actually still learning the business. I had to get educated. And there was only so much I could learn from Mom. Looking back now, I realize I got most of my education in bonds by sitting down, knuckling under, and teaching myself my subject—in the act of getting it down on paper—in the weekly newsletter.

Those newsletters told our clients and prospects what to do with their money. But they were written by me *for me* because I was the first one my own words had to educate. My friend, William K. Zinsser, whose *On Writing Well* going into its seventh edition (HarperCollins, 1976, 1,200,000 copies sold) calls what I do "writing to learn." Zinsser's thesis is that writing is learning. You teach yourself your subject by having to make it picture-clear to others. That is how I made municipal bonds "my babies." Every Friday for 40 years, 2,000 Fridays, I dug into the core of my being and forced myself to get to the bottom of the bond market. But, despite the greasy grind that I became, I never could learn the answer to the $1,845,000,000,000 question (which is the volume of munis outstanding) that everybody wants to know: "Okay Jim, Where are interest rates going?"

I know I don't know. And you know I don't know. But sitting across the desk from a client with a fortune to invest, the trick is never to utter the words, "I don't know," or the old chestnut, "If I knew, we'd both be rich," or worse, "That's the stupidest question I've ever heard." Even though it is. But as Sayra Lebenthal would say, "There are no stupid questions in municipal bonds. Only stupid answers."

Lou Rukeyser once lobbed the question to me on his show *Wall Street Week*. And I took it and ran: "Lou, we both know I don't know, but I'll tell you what I *wish*." Then I went into my spiel about inflation, deflation, recession, depression, the dust belt, the rust belt, productivity, and savings rates in the United States. A tough thing to bring off and still keep your answer down, before Lou has to cut you off to keep his show moving right along.

Not to deprecate myself too much, I say facetiously that, of course, I know where interest rates are going. Because I'm the one who has to inform Lebenthal's printer a year in advance so that the bond illustrations in our sales literature are always on top of the market. Though I'd sooner calculate when a plume of cigarette smoke will suddenly disintegrate into chaotic swirls . . . or the point when you turn the faucet just so and the water pipe in the laundry room will knock and bang and go crazy. Likewise, predicting the rise or fall of interest rates involves situations wherein tiny differences in input can quickly become overwhelming differences in output. It is what

James Gleick in *Chaos: Making a New Science* (Viking Penguin, 1987) refers to as the *Butterfly Effect*. It is the notion that a butterfly stirring the air in Beijing can transform storm patterns the following month in New York.

Just think of all the fluttering butterflies that contribute to the turbulence sending the 10-year Treasury bond ricocheting in one direction or another: the Dow, the dollar, the deficit, deflation, and devastation wrought by 9/11. And those are just things beginning with the letter D.

Interest rates face too many forces, large and small, tugging and pulling in different directions at the same time. How can we petty bond sellers predict where the ten-year bond will be in two weeks, two months, two years from now? And yet, in a roomful of experts, you'll find some saying interest rates are going up, some saying they're not. How do you know who is right? Whomever you agree with. And that is what makes you one of the experts.

Luckily, not every question about interest rates ("How much will I get if I have to sell?") is a request for information. Years ago at the elite progressive Dalton School, we kids used questions as springboards for whatever popped in our heads. So to me, questions about interest rates and "Suppose I have to sell?" and "What if they kill tax exemptions?" could just be conversational gambits. The way I look at it, bond wonks are just being tested for intellectual honesty. So, ask me where interest rates are going, and I might just regale you with other examples of unpredictable, unquantifiable turbulence from Glieck's *Chaos*, like the rise and fall of the anchovy population off the coast of Peru. You are going to have fun doing business with me over the decade to come. Honest!

Bores Need Not Apply

I have a Princeton classmate who went into his family's eyeglass frame business. He has turned those two little OO shaped wires that bestride the bridge of the nose into a calling. He delights in making eyes beautiful. He's got a purpose in life. Beauty! Well, I have a purpose, too. I want to entice people into saving. Then I want them to convert those savings into bonds. Bonds that transform themselves into roads and bridges, tunnels and sewers, schools and subways—genuine productive assets that contribute to jobs and incomes and more savings for everybody. Of course, those bonds must also pay my clients the kind of tax-free income that no bank can give them.

I want salespeople to make the product they are selling interesting. I want you to do what I have done with dull, ordinary municipal bonds and humanize every bootjack and sump pump on the market. Follow my "yellow brick road." Find the connection between things and people. Municipal bonds were once the most boring investment in America, until I came along and said, "My bonds aren't paper. They're the nuts and bolts that make New York work. . . . Love my subway? Love my bonds!" If I could make you love my subway, my sewer, my wastewater treatment plant, think what you can do with sliced bread. I have made a life's work out of looking for the other guy's self-interest, while having my share of happiness and self-fulfillment in the workplace. Often challenging, never boring.

Boredom? What's that? It is low-level motion sickness caused by kelp beds of hairy green spores in your head, teased into swaying to and fro like seaweed, by the empty promise of food for thought that leaves you feeling unfed and empty. The perpetrators of this numbing condition are the bores. Bores can empty a room, kill a party, curtail a night out. But one thing they can't do is sell. Nor can they be trained to sell.

You don't think of George Washington as a salesman. But the early American philosopher Ralph Waldo Emerson commented that when George walked into a room he exuded a force of personality and character that automatically made those around him want to buy whatever he was selling. Washington was no slap-of-the-heel charmer. He was known to be rather stiff and formal. He didn't even go for shaking hands. He bowed. But dammit he had style! And he used that style to sell his product—the United States of America.

The top salesman at Lebenthal & Company has authority, self-assurance, and command. Without hearing him speak a word, one senses the thinking behind any recommendation to come. Could he be about to suggest a zero coupon municipal bond? An immediate pay annuity with the monthly income going to fund the premium on a life insurance policy? A covered call? I wouldn't know. I have barely heard him speak. He is so soft-spoken, my granddaughter Ellie's Pablum would seem like Habanero Hot Sauce by comparison. But when Jeff James pronounces that "life is a fountain," ears perk up. Jeff is memorable. He is *sui generis*.

Would I want a company full of Jeffs? From a P&L (profit and loss) standpoint, sure! But there are 1.4 million CUSIP (Committee on Uniform Securities Identification

Procedures) numbers out there representing 1.4 million combinations of issuer, coupon, and maturity to mix and match with all kinds of potential buyers. And now with more than just municipal bonds for sale at Lebenthal—I won't rule out any personality type from working at our company, other than crooks, liars, cheats—and, God help us, those bores.

Money Has a Life of Its Own

For most of Lebenthal's history, we were in the business of avoiding risk, especially by dealing in the blue chips of the bond business—general obligation municipal bonds—considered second in safety only to U.S. Treasury bonds. But when Lebenthal diversified into stocks, we moved into the business of *managing* risk instead of just avoiding it. The idea of adding stocks to a bond portfolio, or bonds to a stock portfolio, is not just for risk and reward to cancel each other out. Managing risk is the business of trying to increase return without commensurately increasing risk (and conversely trying to reduce risk without commensurately reducing return).

If that sounds too good to be true, tell it to the Nobel Prize Committee. In 1990, they gave Harry Max Markowitz the Nobel Prize in Economics for Modern Portfolio Theory (MPT) and for working out the math of an anomaly. Stocks go up . . . and stocks go down. Bonds go up . . . and bonds go down. But they tend not to go up and down at the same time. Out of which comes the most basic tenet of Modern Portfolio Theory: Diversifying among truly diversifiable asset classes is more important than what mother called "hitting the market," getting in at the bottom, out at the top. What you buy (asset allocation) is more important than when you buy it (market timing). I practice MPT with my money. I'm a believer in time smoothing out short-term volatility. And I invest for the "long haul." I may not be around to enjoy the long haul. But who am I to complain? It is not me, it is my money that counts. And my money, I'm trying to make sure, has a long life of its own.

More than Municipal Bonds, but with the Same Loving Care

I'll admit that at first I was reluctant when Alexandra brought up adding stocks to our quiver. In my mind, breaking the news to our dyed-in-the-wool, 100 percent bond portfolio customers was like explaining that Bill Blass had suddenly turned around and was selling bedsheets and chocolates. I gave the assignment of making the case for both stocks and bonds at Lebenthal to two hypersuccessful iconoclasts from the advertising world, Ron Holland and George Lois.

They summed it up in three incontrovertible sentences to be spoken on TV by Alexandra: "Today it isn't just making money that counts. The trick is holding onto it." And,

"Here comes the New Lebenthal."

I must say something now that I certainly wouldn't say about a man. But I will say it about my own daughter. One look on camera by that savvy kid is worth a thousand words like "Modern Portfolio Theory," "asset allocation," and "diversification," all of them implied silently in a nanosecond by her smile.

One by one, Alexandra added to Lebenthal's larder: stocks, mutual funds, insurance, annuities, long-term care, 529 school savings plans, and financial planning. "More than municipal bonds," she said, "but the same loving care." I wholeheartedly aided and abetted the New Lebenthal. But I told Alexandra that I wasn't going to follow her to the Promised Land. And like Moses, I never have sold my clients a single share of stock (other than XTX, the symbol of the "New York Tax-Exempt Bond Fund, Inc.," the closed end bond fund that Mother once approved).

LEBENTHAL TO GO

When you've made the sale,
say, "Thank you, good-bye!"
And get off the phone.

Everybody knows money isn't funny.
But what's wrong with putting a
recalcitrant client in a good mood
(if it helps close the sale)?

God gave you two ears and one mouth.
Take the hint.

Even if you're dying to
hear your own words,
you'll sell more by listening.

Be fair and always tell customers
enough for them to say,
"yes . . . or no."
If they say no,
don't be too hard on yourself.
That sale was not meant to happen.

Your customers have something
they love very much.
Their money.
The moment I convince them
my bonds are worth more than
their money, a sale is made.

4

Do It! Just Do It, Do It, Do It!

We Are All Lebenthals

It takes a rocking, rolling three minutes for the No. 4 Lexington Avenue subway express train to hurtle a mile and a half from 14th Street up to Grand Central. Yipes! That left me with three minutes and nothing to do. No problem. I gave myself an assignment in make-work: Come up with an ad for MBIA, the insurance company that guarantees payment of municipal bonds. And, lo, it came to pass. Before the train screeched into Grand Central, a headline emerged: *You Will Be Paid.* This promise was the foundation for Lebenthal & Company's blockbuster campaign for "Empire Gtd.," our unit investment trust insured by MBIA, proving: Hey! This guy can think fast!

But how fast was it, after all? I'd been stewing, brewing, and obsessing over municipal bond insurance long be-

48

fore I started playing mind games on that subway ride. By turning riders sitting across the aisle from me into imaginary clients, all of a sudden the promise of municipal bond insurance bubbled up: You Will Be Paid. Bingo! I had my headline.

But ideas don't just pop into my head, "Wham! Bam! Alakazam!" They well up and brim over from this visceral stewpot of thoughts, notions, and meditations that at some point become a gut reaction. I am one of those people with a dominant right brain, who acts on impulse and intuition. I've got a direct connection between my gut feeling and my trigger finger. If it feels right, I do it. I just do it, do it, do it! That is why a gut is a terrible thing to waste.

Listening to the gut and acting on its intuition can sometimes be risky business. But going with the gut has made my company the best known municipal bond firm in the country, and it has allowed me to be "Present at the Creation" over and over again. That is what I call the moment of unveiling, when an advertising agency displays their creation on the conference table like the Child in the manger. So, how do you know if it's great? It glows. It resonates. It makes people in the room exclaim, "Yes! That's it! That's it!" You know they've hit the jackpot. Somehow, you just know.

I was present at the Creation when our ad agency, Isidore Lefkowitz Elgort, uncovered the idea for *We Treat You Like Family,* and released the heady ether of magic marker into the air rising from their rough drawing of a stick figure of the great movie star saying, "I'm Myrna Lebenthal. You May Know Me as Myrna Loy. But to Lebenthal, I'm One of the Family."

Let me ask you: What's the last thing you would want to read in an ad? Guffy, self-serving advertising copy about customer care on Wall Street. Right? Well, "Made you look, made you look, made you buy a penny book." To make the point that looking after people made Lebenthal clients feel like family, Joan Fontaine called herself Joan Lebenthal. Count Basie became Count Lebenthal, Van Johnson appeared as Van Lebenthal, and my college sweetheart June Lockhart was, at least in my ad, June Lebenthal. The reader knew who these recognizable stars really were. So why the name change? That was the magic. You just had to read the copy to find out, and read folks did. The best written endorsement of service and customer care, and an example of suspension of disbelief, since "You have a friend at Chase Manhattan." A clear case of an ad making you say, "I'll bite. Tell me more."

Deeds, Not Words, Lebenthal!

The late, great, and hat-crowned Congresswoman Bella Abzug once singled me out at a street fair and barked, "Deeds, not words." Lebenthal! How do you like that? Right out of the blue. She could only have imagined a crack in my reputation as a man of action. Because when I get an idea, I don't let go, until I turn it into a deed. A good case in point being "minibonds," and how I worked the idea of a small tax-free saving bond for the working man and woman into the ear of the Mayor of New York.

Bella's goading remark from a decade earlier was still lingering, when in 1991 Mayor David Dinkins of New York challenged ordinary New Yorkers, "If you've got a better idea for making New York City work, come on down to City Hall and get it off your chest."

After a comeback from the fiscal crisis of the 1970s under Mayor Ed Koch in the 1980s, once again the City was going through hard times. There was havoc uptown, downtown, everywhere. In our crumbling bridges. In our bombed-out, burned-out ghettos. In human wreckage turned out into the streets. Huge deficits were hanging over the city's head. The rioting between blacks and Hasidim Jews in Crown Heights, Brooklyn, was tearing New Yorkers apart. Dinkins, the city's first black mayor was being blamed—for holding back the police, for letting the feeling once again prevail that New York City was ungovernable and out of control, in a word for being David Dinkins, the City's first black mayor.

So, there was Mayor Dinkins asking for help. And there was I, a Wall Street investment banker who underwrote New York City bonds and well known in City Hall for socking those bonds away in people's portfolios—in $10,000, $25,000, $100,000 blocks—where they would happily sit until maturity and not come back and hang over the market. Lebenthal had been campaigning the powers that be to issue New York City minibonds in $1,000 pieces for the little guy. To broaden the market and undo the bad rap that tax-free municipal bonds were strictly for fat cats and Park Avenue millionaires. We got nowhere . . . until the Mayor extended his famous invitation, "Come on down to City

51

Hall!" No RSVP required. Just get on line, and wait your turn.

Well, Chase's David Rockefeller didn't go.

Citibank's Walter Wriston didn't go.

Bank of New York's J. Carter Bacot didn't go.

But Sayra Lebenthal's boy Jim couldn't wait. I got on line with the little girl, the taxi driver, the songwriter, the hot dog man, the yippie, and 2,200 other New Yorkers to tell Dinkins how to run his city. Most were shuffled upstairs or to the basement to vent with lesser city officials. But as the line moved up the steps of City Hall, an aide recognized me from our Lebenthal TV commercial and asked what I was selling. I told him, "New York City savings bonds in small denominations for the working man." "I'll get you in," he said.

"What are you doing here?" Mayor Dinkins asked me. "You could have picked up the telephone. You could have just called."

"Maybe so, Mr. Mayor. But then I wouldn't have had 19 television crews waiting to interview me to see how I made out in here." The fact is that the next day the idea of "Lebenthal Tax-Free Savings Bond" made page one of the *New York Times.* A *Times* editorial inside called them "Little Bonds for the Big City" and predicted they would create a new cadre of committed New Yorkers, by giving the little guy a sense of ownership and financial stake in the well-being of the city.

Mayor Dinkins flipped about the idea and ordered me in front of the cabinet members around his desk, "Keep talking with these guys, work it out." A year later, Lebenthal was marketing minibonds to the masses, a small denomination tax-free zero coupon bond called the "NYC Bond", and plastering the subways with ads shouting, "Put $1,000 in. Get $2,000 out. And pay no tax."

Deeds, Lebenthal, deeds. Belicose Bella was right. Action always speaks louder than words.

I Know What, Let's Put on a Show

When teachers hand out homework in school, they don't warn you that writing is hard work. For me, one letter, one word, one sentence at a time slows down my "if you see something, say something" process. Give me the spoken word any day. Talking is easier than writing because, for me, cognition and articulation happen nanoseconds apart, and the words just come rolling off my restless tongue. But for the ultimate shorthand right into the other guy's viscera—Bam! Bam!—there is nothing like a television commercial, with sight and sound, words, and—the most sensual appeal to the senses—music. I figured that's just what it would take—"Music Maestro!"—to undo the perception of municipal bonds as just a rich man's plaything when 20-year old munibond guys in Gucci loafers and $1,000 suits started brandishing their $25 Havana cigars on the cover of *Fortune* magazine. With deficits to close, with fairness and tax reform in the air, and with the prevailing popular impression of a dowager in her parlor clipping coupons with gilded scissors and paying no tax,

Congress was determined to tax anything that walked, talked, or looked the slightest like a loophole. Tax free municipal bonds were in hot water.

So up Madison Avenue I walked, across 57th Street, into the advertising agency, Wells Rich Greene. They had produced the most successful commercial of all time for the New York State Chamber of Commerce, using the song, "I Love New York." Like Ray Charles singing, "America the Beautiful," "I Love New York," goes right to the soul. The song (words and music by Steve Karmen) actually turned the morale of New York City around.

As I stepped into the office, I asked the receptionist, "Who do I see? I think I need a song."

"Oh, you mean Charlie Moss? Do you have an appointment?"

"No, Miss, but I thought I'd make one now."

"Charlie," I told him. "I am an ambassador without portfolio of the Public Securities Association. I have no budget. They don't even know I'm here. But munis are under the gun, and we've got to save them."

That's why I love the idea of advertising agencies. You tell them your problem. You go away. You come back in two or three weeks. And, if you're lucky, there, on the wall, in the air, glowing on the conference table is the fire they have stolen from the gods. In this instance, it was the song "Built by Bonds," with that same Steven Karmen's words and music, and pictures of the mighty public works built by tax-free municipal bonds. From under the noses of the muses, Karmen again had stolen and reincarnated the soul . . . of a thing . . . called a municipal bond.

The reason you can't hum "Built by Bonds" or even remember the words is because the commercial, although it did get made, never saw the light of day. My industry, God bless us, is made up of masters of the deal, rational, logical, computational but too focused on the trees to see the forest. It is called impaired abstract thinking, the inability to see how what we do fits into the grander scheme of things. For only 10-cents out of every $1,000 worth of bonds issued in 1987, they could have had a $10,000,000 campaign that would have convinced the politicians, the public, and the press that "Built by Bonds" was as true as "Things Go Better With Coke."

Oh, there is so much injustice in the world. Well, at last a little of it blew my way. For the commercial that never ran and my efforts to show that you can't get up in the morning, take a shower, a subway, a bus, go over the bridge, or under the river, without a municipal bond touching your life, I was awarded the Public Securities Association's First Annual Chairman's Achievement Award. Give that man the same grade I got at Andover in Latin: 60 with an A for effort (Superlative, Jim, more than can humanly be expected). In other words, nice try, Jim!

"Foul! Fraud! Unconscionable! Breach of Contract! Breach of Faith!" (Now, Who's Getting Emotional?)

I was bottle-fed on the sanctity of contracts. My daily Pablum was the safety record of municipal bonds after the

Great Chicago Fire, the San Francisco Earthquake, the Galveston Hurricane and Flood, and the first hurricane that obliterated New Orleans in 1926. Fed on those tales of municipal honor and valor at birth, I was ingrained to loathe the early issuers of canal and railroad development bonds who, when things didn't pan out, turned their pockets inside out and just walked away from their bonded debt. When the mentors doing the ingraining are your own Mom and Dad, it is a natural function of the right brain to get emotional and take default and repudiation of bond debt personally.

So, there you see me in the early 1980s standing at a blackboard in a TV commercial about some big, beautiful New York City Housing Development 12¾ percent bonds, synchronizing tossing a piece of chalk in the air and catching it, while saying, "They can't tax it, and they can't take it away from you the minute interest rates come down." Bonds are always being called just when you wish they wouldn't. But the beautiful thing about the HDC 12¾s was that they could not be called for ten years.

Well, shut my mouth, if the HDC didn't throw my words in my teeth. They suddenly announced they were redeeming the bonds six years ahead of the permissible call date. There were extraordinary situations in which the bonds could be redeemed prematurely. In this case however, the "Preliminary Official Statement" disclosing the terms of the deal, had specifically said the bonds could not be called from "recoveries of principal" from the opportunistic sale of the mortgages underlying the bonds. But, without a sticker or heads-up warning of any kind, the "Final Official Statement" delivered with the bonds said just the opposite. So, as interest rates came down, HDC sold out the mortgages and used those very "recoveries of principal" to redeem their bonds at par, par being 100. (Just before the call, those big, beautiful 12¾s had been fetching 122 in the open market.)

"Unconscionable! Foul! Sharp practices! Confiscation of property! Illegal!" I fulminated. But I don't just fulminate. I sue. ("Deeds, Lebenthal, not words!") I turned into the Righteous Avenger instigating multiple lawsuits against HDC for breach of contract, and breach of faith, and securities fraud, and common law fraud.

The Bank Of New York brought the action on behalf of a bondholder. Who else but our Empire State Municipal Exempt Trust? And after two long years we won.

Obviously, it was too late to call off the call, but the court threw us a bone: A modicum in damages and, more important, a cease and desist order on the next round of calls HDC had been contemplating for its 8⅞ths.

Was I too passionate? Pawing the earth? Clawing the air? Putting up my dukes. "You wanna fight? You wanna fight?" Au contraire, Jim, said the National Federation of Municipal Analysts in awarding me their lifetime achievement Award in 2002 for passion and remarkable dedication to the municipal bond industry. Sticking to my guns (and having them in the first place) sure made selling municipal bonds for my mother more stimulating than Hollywood.

How Eight Little Girls
Made the Sun Come Up

Fighting the good fight to hold a bond issuer's feet to the fire began with the New York City Fiscal Crisis of 1975.

To pay for its daily operations, New York City had been borrowing left and right against future tax and revenue receipts that had dubious chances of ever materializing—and then borrowing anew from B to pay off its debt to A.

I remember, if nobody else does, February 28, 1975, the day the jig was up. Bankers Trust had been high bidder on a city tax anticipation note. Bankers' bankers arrived at the Municipal Bonding with their law firm, White and Case in tow and a $100 million settlement check in hand. Before handing over the money, however, the lawyers wanted to see if the city was within its legal borrowing authority.

An audit showed that the city had been borrowing far beyond its legal authority. So the note sale was canceled and Bankers Trust withheld its $100 million. With the city's own credit all but dried up, it was off to Washington we go, hat in hand, begging an unsympathetic Gerald Ford to back a New York City bond issue with a federal guarantee.

"Ford to New York—Drop Dead!" That classic headline on the front page of the *Daily News* said it all. Even Bill Simon, Secretary of the Treasury, scoffed, "Let the City default. The sun will still rise in the morning." I knew it was time to set somebody straight on exactly who and precisely how many would get hurt in a New York City default. So, one Saturday, I enlisted eight of my daughter Alexandra's fifth-grade classmates at St. Hilda's to come to Lebenthal & Company and count years of Lebenthal's bond transactions to determine how many of flesh-and-blood ordinary citizens owned New York City bonds. Based on the kids' tabulations and our share of the market, I could confidently extrapolate into written testimony for the Senate Committee holding hearings on federal aid for New York City that overall 160,000 folks owned $4,895,000,000 of the $7,350,000,000 of NYC bonds outstanding.

Through our weekly newsletter, we exhorted reticent New York City bond owners to come out of hiding and tell the press, the public, and the United States Senate, "Those are my savings, Mr. President." The words of those everyday investors put default into human terms. And those tiny tugs on the heart strings did the trick. (Remember: in a dead calm, on a windless day, with no current, no tide, and no viscosity of water, even a child could tug the QE2 to shore with a number 10 thread.) The Senate came through with a bailout. And the sun did rise on November 4, 1975, for 160,000 bondholders, although not with a complete smiley face. New York City had to declare a "Moratorium" on the repayment of one billion dollars worth of its municipal notes. "Can we do that?" asked Governor Hugh Carey? "No!" his legal advisors said. But the moratorium would go to court and that would buy time for the City to get its act together.

The moratorium bought one other thing for New York City: Treasury Secretary Simon's nod of approval for the federal loan guarantee to help the City over its immediate liquidity crisis. Demonic as it sounds, Simon's price for bailing out the city was public humiliation of New York City for its prodigal ways. The moratorium was his way of rubbing New York's nose in it.

In a year, thanks to the suit of a bondholder, the court would strike down the moratorium, and "Big MAC"—the Municipal Assistance Corporation—would pay off the city's notes. At long last, financially speaking, New York was straightening up and flying right and soon would become the model for other cities of the fiscal sinner reformed.

At the time Alexandra's little classmates were doing their part in saving the day—the problem for me was how show them thanks. Aha! When installing new call directors for the office, the telephone company had left behind a coil of thick unused cable, packed inside with beautiful multicolored wires. I cut the stuff in 4-inch sections and presented each little girl with a piece of plastic coated wire, which I dubbed "Ma Bell Wampum," more desirable to those 11 year olds, more intrinsically valuable, than money, any day.

It's the little things that count. In this case, it was Alexandra's four-foot-tall classmates literally counting thousands of bond owners.

The Securities and Exchange Commission and the Place Mat for My Tuna on Rye

I am a booster. I am positive and upbeat. I want to please everybody. So, I am always taken aback when I fail and my motherhood-and-apple-pie approach runs into opposition. Naturally, I was disappointed when Sam Donaldson on ABC's *Prime Time Live* threw me a zinger akin to "when did I stop beating my wife?" and challenged me with "Why should the rich not pay income tax just because they can afford municipal bonds?" I was dismayed, when the *New York Times* reported "a worried investor's concerns, 'Does anyone honestly believe the politicians who run New York City not going to pay policemen and firemen in order to pay interest to bondholders?' I was crushed when *Forbes* magazine sneered in a bold face headline **Lebenthal & Co.: Heroes To Whom?. . . Certainly to Abe Beame, but not to all its customers,"** and called Lebenthal & Company "a brassy little firm."

But I really knew I was in dutch, when the industry's regulatory body, the Securities and Exchange Commission (SEC), issued Lebenthal & Company an official call to the carpet, a Subpoena *Ducus Tecum,* meaning come see us and bring with you everything you have written in those ads and newsletters promoting New York City bonds.

I spent eight endless hours of grilling during the SEC's investigation into the sale of New York City bonds. Much of the time was spent rehashing a full-page Lebenthal ad that we had run in the *New York Times* on April 4, 1975, two days after Standard & Poor's suspended their rating on New York City bonds. The headline shouted:

The Second Safest Investment in America
Bondholders must be paid by law. Before the policemen. Before the firemen. Before welfare recipients. Even before the mayor.

. . . paying bondholders has priority over all other municipal obligations.

. . . general obligation bonds—including New York City's—are the second safest investment in America—second only to U.S. Government bonds.

. . . losing confidence in New York—second only to losing confidence in America.

The SEC investigator was incredulous. Where'd you get this stuff, Lebenthal?

Out of my mouth and into my testimony under oath came the answer: "From basic bond lore learned at the breast."

What else could I say? That I had really learned about "prior lien" from a laminated promotion piece on New York City bonds from long out of business bond firm that I used as a table mat for my tuna on rye at the trading desk in my earliest days in the bond business.

Coffee stains and cigarette burns notwithstanding, that plastic doily drummed into my head that under Article VIII, Section 2, of the constitution of the state of New York bondholders get paid first!

"If at any time, the respective appropriating authorities shall fail to make such appropriation (for debt service), a sufficient sum shall be set apart from the first revenues thereafter received and shall be applied to such purpose."

I would quote Article VIII, Section 2 in Lebenthal ads. The Mayor and City Comptroller would quote me. And then I would turn around and paraphrase what the Mayor and Comptroller had said: "As the holder of a New York City bond, you get yours before policemen, firemen, teachers, or welfare recipients get theirs."

I knew I was caught in the turbulence of mutual feedback when Mayor Abe Beame held the "Second Safest Investment in America" ad high over his head with both hands and told the elite of the financial analyst community at a Money Marketeers dinner, "See, Lebenthal says our bonds are good." It wasn't long after that the city went broke, the notes defaulted, I became the laughingstock of the investment world, the subpoena arrived from the SEC, and we were hiring the best lawyers money could buy to prepare my defense against possible charges of fraud, market manipulation, false advertising, and even worse, for an ex-journalist, unabashed gushing and enthusiasm.

By the time the SEC investigated and published its findings—condemning the entire bond industry for failure to perform due diligence and swallowing the city's word, hook, line, and sinker (nothing about me personally, thank God))—the court of appeals had already overturned the moratorium and told the city to pay up. Hardship is no defense. "A pledge of the city's faith and credit is both a commitment to pay and a commitment of the city's revenue generating powers to produce the funds to pay."

Article VIII, Section 2, "prior lien," "Second Safest Investment in America," and enthusiastic I had won the day.

The Friday night of the court's decision, I had finished recording an announcement for our answering machine. I knew clients would be phoning in over the weekend for our reaction and asking what to do next with their NYC notes. I think I would have told them—28 years ago—a seawall is all the stronger for having been repaired! I think I would have told callers: Now that New York City bonds were all the stronger for their legal obligation to pay having been reaffirmed, if folks didn't need their cash, they should roll over their notes into longer term city bonds. But after 28 years, I cannot be sure.

All I know is that I was turning off the lights in the office and letting the lights of New York, New York, twinkle and sparkle in the dark outside, when the night line rang. I answered. It was the SEC investigator who had dragged me over the coals but also chastened me about taste, the need for striking a tone of fairness and balance in financial advertising.

What an amazing turnaround! Tonight he was calling and asking for my thoughts. What did I think would happen to the city now that it had to pay while its cupboard was still bare? Would note holders jam the window fighting for the last dollar in the city's till and force the city into bankruptcy? Should the SEC suspend trading in NYC paper?

"You know me," I said, "I love to talk. But do you really expect me to without a lawyer?"

Did I talk and tell him what I thought would happen when the market opened on Monday? Or did I say, "Please hang up, call back, and wait three rings for my recorded announcement?" That's sure what I would tell him to do today. After all, the short recorded telephone message, the

30-second spot, punchy headlines—like "You Will Be Paid," "They Can't Tax It or Take It Away from You the Minute Interest Rates Come Down," "We Treat You Like Family,"—are my way, the Lebenthal way, of talking and, no matter how brief the message, speaking volumes.

LEBENTHAL TO GO

A good ad makes you say the following
things: I didn't know that.
I'll bite. Tell me more.

When the reason to do something
equals the reason not to do it,
I'd say, "Just do it," every time.

I'll say it again, "Effort is no
guarantee of success. It's just a
license to keep on truckin'."

Give a damn! You have no idea
where it will lead you.

If you stick your neck out,
you're going to get it in the neck.
That's what necks are for.

5

This I Believe

Hrrumph!

As mayor I've cut costs $2.8
billion, and New York City still
faces its biggest budget gap ever.

(Mayor Bloomberg speech December 7, 2002,
at CBC Conference in New York City "How
New York City Should Close Its Budget Gap")

Here we go again.

This time it is Mayor Michael Bloomberg's turn to stand
in front of the Citizen's Budget Commission with furrowed
brow. I ask myself how many more fiscal crises do I have to
sit through in a lifetime?

... the law requires us to close this gap and balance the budget. There are simply no alternatives. Our expenses and revenues have to be the same.

My mind is off in the clouds as I contemplate the connections between our economic well-being and the bridges that leap over obstacles to traffic and commerce, mass transit that gets people to work on time, solid waste facilities that plow our leftovers into useful form, housing that makes you happy to live and work in this City on the Hill.

A $2.8 billion shortfall is not something we can just grow our way out of.

I come back to earth. I am not supposed to be building castles in the air. We realistic municipal bond men are supposed to be telling you that California has a liquidity crisis, tobacco bonds are not out of the woods, declining market values can wipe out everything you have earned if interest rates climb back to the moon. What am I doing daydreaming away while all these businessmen stroke their beards?

Dear Diary!

The answer to my thoughts is in a storeroom only 1,000 feet from Ground Zero, at Lebenthal's offices, in downtown Manhattan. For 42 years, I poured my guts into our weekly Lebenthal newsletter—what I think, what I feel, what I really believe in. Everything from my reaction when the Fed tightened the screws the other day to my absolute delight and sheer pride in the municipal bond issue Lebenthal underwrote for Glen Rock Senior Citizen Housing:

> Their hearts were young and gay. And so is their
> life today. They're not in a nursing home.
> They're not shunted off to a mountaintop.
> They're right where they belong. They're in the
> Glen Courts—Glen Rock, New Jersey's Senior
> Citizen Houses—in the area where
> they grew up, raised families, and led a full life.

Rows and rows of those newsletters of mine are archived for posterity and not just ego. The National Association of Securities Dealers (NASD) regulations require it. But whenever I want to, I can hole up on a rainy afternoon in my old age, and bring back to life whatever was going on any time from 1964 right up to today. In the economy and the bond business that I thought was so right, so wrong, so funny, so nutty, so terrible—but always so important—at the time.

I'm No Eleanor Roosevelt, But . . .

In the 1950s, the incomparable radio and television newsman, Edward R. Murrow, asked great and famous people from all walks of life to look into their hearts and write a 3-minute essay about what they believed and why. And for four years, Murrow's radio program, *This I Believe,* starred men and women like Helen Keller, Thomas Mann, Eleanor Roosevelt, and Jackie Robinson reading their straight from the heart personal statements. *This I Believe,* was one of the most listened to broadcasts on the air. I always listened in awe and admiration, just imagining what it must be like trying to write what you believe—without preaching, boring, or conning yourself. I wondered, "Could I do that without pontificating or getting up on my high horse?" With the bar for intellectual honesty set that high, I never really tried to play the game. Until this minute.

As I said once in the opening of a speech, "If any of you in the back are trying to sleep, please keep the snoring down, because I'm dying to hear what I have to say." So, while I'm no Eleanor Roosevelt, I would still love to hear what I have to say about my own philosophy. Fortunately (for the slow writer in me, scratching his head at the keyboard), my philosophy is already on record in these newsletters, my love letters to Lebenthal clients, nine of which follow in making the claim that, "This I Believe."

Lebenthal & Co., Inc.

MUNICIPAL
BONDS
FOR THE
INDIVIDUAL
INVESTOR

A Funny Thing Is Happening

I am beginning to feel about my City the way most people are taught to feel about their Country. It is a form of Patriotism, like loving the flag and amber waves of grain. Only scaled down and concentrated on the town I live in.

What gets me is the obscenity of the anti-people people. Not the profane tantrums of Abbie Hoffman kicking his shoes off at the shins of Miss Liberty. I mean the obscene hypocrisy of my fellow Athenians who will extend easy come feelings of goodwill to the Country, but do not give a fig for the parts of the whole where the problems have come to roost. They curse the cities, they curse the mayor, they curse the firemen, they curse the cabbies, they curse the poor, they curse the rudeness, they curse the litter, they curse the taxes, they curse the night, they curse the day—only adding to the sum of human decay they profess to lament.

The point is this.

It's nice to have a dacha in the Hamptons. But the United States of America is New York City. And New York City is the United States of America.

January 8, 1971   Lebenthal

Lebenthal & Co., Inc.

MUNICIPAL
BONDS
FOR THE
INDIVIDUAL
INVESTOR

Scaring the Fish Away

Last Week in Pennsylvania a group of businessmen and their guests gathered at fishing camp to open trout season, which cannot be done without a certain amount of howling at the moon. But no sooner were the rods assembled than the conversation turned to how welfare, inflation, and long hair were ruining the country. Or was it the war, social irresponsibility, and the worship of the almighty buck? The vociferizing had entered the free fire zone where anybody who talks is shot down.

Something is missing from the rhetoric these days. A common point of departure. The hardheaded businessman talks of preservation of the dollar and economic responsibility. The bleeding heart humanitarian talks about democratic ideals and the power to the people as if these were ends in themselves. The arguments of both are frail and wither in the presence of each other's opposition without a common point of departure: some agreement about what kind of balance we want to strike between the pleasures of the individual and the needs of the community which is the source of individual opportunity in the first place.

How to make the owner of the coal mine in Pennsylvania see that the problem of the cities is America's heart trouble and not just a carbuncle on the neck of the nation? How to make the liberal minded city dweller see that the mine safety bill with all its humanitarian objectives is going to raise the price of the cool air soughing through the vents this summer?

Wanted. A big concept that will tie you to me and me to you and both of us to the whole, and help the pieces fall into place. Until then all the blithering is just scaring the fish away.

April 23, 1971   Lebenthal

Lebenthal & Co., Inc.

MUNICIPAL
BONDS
FOR THE
INDIVIDUAL
INVESTOR

More on Municipals

There is precious little provision in law for the default of a general obligation Municipal Bond—just as there is no provision in the Constitution of the United States for surrendering in war.

It's not allowed.

It's unthinkable.

It's the ultimate defeat.

Yet here we are on the Eve of an excruciatingly long Labor Day weekend of suspense with the word default ringing in every ear. And nobody knowing where the money to avoid default will come from. Yet the attitude prevailing that the money will somehow materialize, just you wait and see.

We too believe that New York City bonds will pay their interest and principal on time, and not just because the Law is adamant or because paying bondholders is the sole purpose of government.

The strongest reason for New York City not defaulting is a practical one:

The garbage has to be hauled. Kids have to have schools to go to. Police have to preserve the peace and public safety.

In short, New York City has to survive. But in order to survive in a capital society, any government or financial institution must be able to borrow.

A perfect payment record is the only means by which New York City can hope to regain its borrowing power and fulfill its role of The Government to 7,800,000 human beings.

August 29, 1975   Lebenthal

Lebenthal & Co., Inc.

MUNICIPAL
BONDS
FOR THE
INDIVIDUAL
INVESTOR

Only the Highest Yields Ever

If inflation is too much money chasing too few goods, it follows that the attack on inflation has got to come from two directions: (1) Reduce the money supply. (2) Increase productivity, so more goods and services exist relative to the amount of money around.

Stop thinking of money as just greenbacks coming off a press. The kind of money at the root of inflation evil is bank credit. When you borrow from the bank and start issuing checks, those checks become deposits at a bank somewhere else. And those deposits become new loans that become new deposits that become new loans, and on and on. They say that every dollar borrowed from the commercial banking system reproduces itself this way seven times.

So the Federal Reserve in its attack on inflation via monetary policy is trying to halt the runaway growth of this super-money, bank credit, by letting interest rates go to the moon, if that's what it takes to restrain the excessive growth of money and credit.

Last week, Iacocca called it "madness." Detroit's November auto sales were down 19% from October. October housing permits were off 15%—the very conditions that cool the demand for credit and result in interest rates coming down on their own accord.

If high interest rates as a matter of government policy are like rabies shots that hurt as bad as the disease, there's always the other way at the problem of inflation. Improve productivity.

If as a nation we ever do remove the disincentives to productivity and ever do increase the amount of goods and services relative to the amount of money around, inflation and interest rates should come down. And those bonds that you are buying today should appreciate in market value.

Meanwhile, if you have the strength and fortitude to buy in this volatile and uncertain market, you must content yourself with a current income of 9% . . . 10% . . . 11%, and more—tax free—only the highest Municipal Bond Yields in the history of our country.

December 5, 1980   Lebenthal

Lebenthal & Co., Inc.

MUNICIPAL
BONDS
FOR THE
INDIVIDUAL
INVESTOR

Ensign Lebenthal

Newport, Rhode Island. Friday, November 30. On only two occasions in the twenty or so years I have been writing the Lebenthal newsletter have I written it in first person singular and signed it Jim Lebenthal. ("I Like Capitalism," January 18, 1974, and "What I'm Telling My Own Mother about Custody and Sweeps Now That We Clear through Morgan Stanley," October 24, 1989.) And today makes three times, with the graduation of my son Jimmy from Officer Candidate School and his commissioning in the United States Navy as Ensign Lebenthal.

Why does a kid, Princeton Class of 1990, a true individual, a scholar, a jock, politician, diplomat, who was President of Cap and Gown, and who with the name Lebenthal could go into the family bond business and have it made, instead choose public service in such arduous form, and commit to five long years in the Navy's Nuclear Submarine Program? A calling? Sense of mission? The Uniform? He does it because he knows what he wants: nuclear submarines. It's as simple as that.

Patriotism, public service, confidence in his own individuality, leadership, commitment, "Princeton in the Nation's Service," discipline, dedication, all those good things just go with the route.

As Jimmy and his shipmates from Menominee, Michigan; Midlothian, Virginia; Omaha, Nebraska; Ravenna, Ohio; Americus, Georgia; Midland, Texas; Buffalo, New York; Medford, Oregon and from everywhere else (including a former Vietnamese boat child who not so many years ago had been plucked from the sea by the U.S. Navy) were sworn in to defend Constitution and Country, I can't tell you the joy of being able to say I am an American.

November 30, 1990   Lebenthal

Lebenthal & Co., Inc.
MUNICIPAL
BONDS
FOR THE
INDIVIDUAL
INVESTOR

Are You Doing Better than Your Parents?
Will Your Kids Do Better than You?

Saving is how one generation takes care of the next. And in that department this generation has dropped the ball.

For the first time in American history your kids cannot automatically look forward to what used to be a national birthright—each generation enjoying a higher standard of living than the last one.

We're not just talking about leaving heirs a big estate. We're talking about leaving them a big America with the tools of production for wringing more goods and services out of the economy for every ounce of effort and hour of time that goes in.

But we don't save enough. Therefore we don't invest enough. Therefore we don't rebuild and replace enough. And that deprives whoever comes next of the seed corn this country needs to grow.

And if we do save? Your unspent income becomes factories, housing, roads, airports—the tools of production for creating jobs and generating income. That's money to spend . . . and save . . . and invest anew, starting the process of renewal and replenishment all over again.

No economic activity by individuals acting in their own self-interest has as much impact on the nation's economic well-being as saving. Putting money away. Not just in a cookie jar or under the mattress, but in technology, innovation and training. Productive assets that create real wealth—and pay off for you and yours for years to come.

It's called the American Dream. Where each generation has a shot. And it all begins with saving. It's not how much you earn that counts. It's how much you save.

May 13, 1994   Lebenthal

Lebenthal & Co., Inc.

MUNICIPAL
BONDS
FOR THE
INDIVIDUAL
INVESTOR

Bringing History Home

I'm thinking of the "We Do Our Part" sticker with the Blue Eagle glued to the window of Lebenthal's office, 14 floors above the street. And it brings back the Depression for me. I'm thinking of the Normandie lying on its side in the Hudson where it caught fire and capsized. And it brings back World War II. The feeblest connections personalize catastrophe and make us spectators feel like more than just bit players in history.

In 1934, my Nurse Rita took me to the beach to watch the Morro Castle burn and run aground off Asbury Park, N.J. In 1937, mother woke me up to come to the window and watch the Hindenburg fly over 815 Park Avenue on the way to its fate in Lakehurst.

I'm thinking about an almanac Dad put together in the 'Thirties of disasters through which Municipal Bonds kept right on paying, illustrated with little drawings of tornado, flood, and fire. Those icons of the flawless safety record of municipal bonds in the face of calamity connect me to the devastation at the World Trade Center site, and give me my authority to predict how municipal bonds will fare in the aftermath of 9/11.

The attack has me thinking about Pearl Harbor. I had just finished reading Kenneth Robert's Rabble in Arms and was coming out of my room in the little kids dorm at Andover for dinner when someone in the hallway said, "Pearl Harbor's been bombed." I'm thinking where I was when I heard about the A-bomb: McCosh Walk, Princeton. I'm thinking about covering a tornado for Life Magazine in 1955 that wiped out Udall, Kansas. 83 dead, 270 injured, 192 buildings destroyed. "Udall is no more," I filed from a Western Union in Wichita. Udall was rebuilt in a year. Today, after 39 years in the Municipal Bond business I know better. Towns that fall down don't stay down.

I'm thinking about the otter movie I produced for Walt Disney and the beavers that, night after night, built their dams. And day after day, the game wardens came and tore the dams down. Build, rebuild. Build, rebuild. It has me thinking about Sisyphus rolling the rock again and again to the top of the mountain, the repeated rebuilding of the Temple, and the mandate babies are born with to breath in, breathe out, and for life to go on. I'm thinking of Dad and the ad he ran in the New York Times in December 1931 saying, "This is no time to let go of your municipal bonds; the municipality has to continue, it cannot run away."

I am surrounded by the memorabilia of Lebenthal's 75 years of converting people's savings into the nuts and bolts that make New York City work—through four wars, 11 recessions, the 1975 NYC Fiscal Crisis, the Great Inflation, and crisis after crisis—and I'm thinking. You can't get up in the morning, flick on a switch, take a shower, a subway, a bus, go over a bridge or under the river without a Municipal Bond touching your life. I'm thinking about New York City going on and on and its bonds going on and on. And having been personally connected so long, I'm thinking about the obligation of our cities to continue providing for the continuation of life. The durability of New Yorkers and the durability of their bonds are one and the same.

September 21, 2001   Lebenthal

Lebenthal & Co., Inc.

MUNICIPAL
BONDS
FOR THE
INDIVIDUAL
INVESTOR

Guess Who's Back in the Saddle on a High Horse Again?

There's nothing wrong with California that a change in human nature won't fix. Who likes to pay taxes? And why do without government services, when you can borrow to pay for them instead? Everybody wants a little something for nothing.

So on July 29, the California Legislature finally passed a budget for FY 2003–2004 that authorizes $98.2 billion in spending—to be paid for with only $72.2 billion of actual revenues from the General Fund. That leaves a hole of $26 billion in the budget to be plugged with $18 billion of deferrals, gimmicks, and massive "Bond Borrowings," and $8 billion that won't be plugged at all. That means 2004–2005 will start on day one with an $8 billion shortfall.

Deficit financing is the bane of capitalism. Now don't get us wrong. We love debt . . . but only when it builds things that make everybody's life better: freeways and tunnels, schools and waterworks, all those projects "Built By Bonds," as we call them, that contribute to economic growth and well-being for years to come.

A community can borrow all day long for capital improvements without watering down its ability to pay, as long as the public debt adds to the productive assets of the community. But when our great American cities and states borrow for current operating expenses, as California plans to do, it's just like Farmer Brown sitting down, tucking in his bib, and devouring the seed corn. It's killing the laying hens for fried chicken. It's slaughtering the breeding cow for steak. It's simply handing future taxpayers the bill for today's expendables, plus cost of interest, with nothing to show for the money once spent.

It has been so long since we've had a good, scary, self-inflicted NYC fiscal crisis or WPPSS default, that even Lebenthal's sense of indignation has been dulled by the apparent permanence of good times. The California budget is just what it takes to shake the complacency and get us back on the high horse setting the State of California straight.

Deficit financing not only makes expendables more expensive. It's addictive and leads to ever growing deficit financing. We're not worried about California defaulting. We're worried about the loss of market value, uninsured California G.O.s trading today at 99 . . . 97 . . . 96 . . . trading tomorrow at 95 . . . 94 . . . 93 . . . . At some level the cost of borrowing alters human nature and tells even politicians they've gotta balance income and outgo by raising taxes and/or cutting expenses.

A funny thing about credit learned in the 1975 NYC Fiscal Crisis. Even sovereigns need their credit to survive. Or who'd lend them money in the first place?

California's survival depends on market access, if only to borrow from B to repay A. So, when the price of money finally tells the legislature, "Uh oh! Credit's drying up," the lowest rated state in the Union will have to straighten up and fly right. At that point uninsured California G.O.s will be a screaming buy.

August 3, 2003   Lebenthal

Lebenthal & Co., Inc.

MUNICIPAL
BONDS
FOR THE
INDIVIDUAL
INVESTOR

The Last Word on Fame (Well, Minor Celebrity)

There I was, night after night, in TV's glorious, living color, doing my noble stuff in millions of New York's bedrooms. In one spot, I poked around our vast sewer system and reminded viewers, "Love my bonds, love my sewers." In another, I deftly caught a tossed peanut in my mouth, after wondering why anybody'd settle for "peanuts," instead of getting supermoney . . . the triple-tax-free income from my municipals.

Well, a funny thing happened on the way to my clients' bedrooms. In the movies, the audience makes you a star, an impossibly remote figure, to be held in awe. TV celebrity is a different ballgame. You're part of the furniture, an everyday item, and you become, just as I had asked them to be, one of the family. So I was not only a relative . . . but one they had loaned their money to. Of course they knew me, and could speak their mind to me. And did they!

Fine by me! I loved losing my privacy, being yelled to by New Yorkers everywhere I went: "How're your babies, Jim?" "What's your bond-of-the-day, Jim?" "Been in any good sewers, lately? Heh! Heh!"

But all the while, I knew that all it took was a goof, a glitch, a clerical error, a late interest check, a surprise new fee, lip from a broker, or failure to drum into a customer's head that bonds go up and bonds go down, and all that city-wide love would go down the drain. Because this meant that their old pal Jim Lebenthal, the guy as comfortable as an old shoe, is now the guy they'll take it out on. Here's what I mean by sticking it to the old man, this typical low blow from someone's high moral ground:

Dear Mr. Lebenthal: July 17, 1992

I couldn't restrain myself from writing you in disgust and anger at your constant plea. Why throw your money away?

Is paying taxes throwing money away? How can our country run without taxes? Or do you only want the working class to pay taxes?

For shame! Is there no place for patriotism and love of helping others? No wonder the country is in the shape it is.

Sadly, I.L.

Dear I.L.:

Ouch! I always thought helping our cities and towns borrow for public necessities in the low cost tax-free bond market was helping everyone out in their capacity as local taxpayers. But I'm not the one who made municipal bonds tax free. Congress did, with the blessing of the courts:

"Anyone may arrange his affairs so that his taxes shall be as low as possible; he is not bound to choose that pattern which best pays the treasury. There is not even a patriotic duty to increase one's taxes. Over and over again the Courts have said that there is nothing sinister in so arranging affairs as to keep taxes as low as possible. Everyone does it, rich and poor alike and all do right, for nobody owes any public duty to pay more than the law demands."—I couldn't put it any better than Judge Learned Hand did in *Helvering v. Gregory,* 69 F.2d 809, 810–11 (2d Cir. 1934).

Best and Regards, Jim Lebenthal

I loved the license being on TV gave me to give back as good as I got. Sure, if I could have written the one-size-fits-all "Gee, I'm sorry you feel that way" form letter, I would have. But, I never did get it quite right, and took every complaint as a chance to reach out and touch somebody personally. Thanks, everybody. Keep those letters and cards coming.

February 17, 2006   Lebenthal

6

Living with Surprise and Loving It

What Did You Do in the War, Daddy?

"What a joy to have Jimmy in our class!" chirped my fourth-grade school report from the Dalton School.

See? Even then, I was a joy to have around. If you don't believe it's true I have my army records for proof:

Dear Corporal Lebenthal:
I have had many opportunities to observe your . . . cheerfulness . . . and consider it very unfortunate that our Table of Distribution and Army-wide freeze precluded promoting you to the grade you warranted.

Sincerely,
Col. Raymond W. Rumph,
Chief of Staff,
Eastern Army Antiaircraft Command

Cheerfulness? In the army? What could I possibly have done in the war, you ask, to deserve such an unmartial commendation?

Which war? The War war? Or the war on the Hollywood movie beat? At the height of the Korean War, I was drafted and immediately sent overseas (to Coney Island). Alright, to nearby Fort Tilden, where in the shadow of the Steeplechase ride and the Parachute Jump, 66-foot-long World War I coastal artillery guns had once looked eagerly out to sea. In 1951, they were long gone, replaced by the 90mm antiaircraft guns of the 69th AAA Gun Battalion, with its command center in the abandoned bunkers under the dunes. We rolled antiaircraft guns out to the end of Long Island and, for practice, aimed our shells at a huge sleeve being towed at the end of a cable attached to a cargo plane, lumbering way out over the ocean. What a blast! Not just the deafening noise of antiaircraft fire. But the hysteria and cries of "Stop the firing!" when the radar started creeping up the steel cable and the actual "bursting of bombs in air," got closer and closer to the tow craft.

When target practice was over, I had the cushy assignment of guarding the battalion's sheets and bedding. That involved riding back to the barracks in a 2½-ton truck, lying back like a sultan with my hands behind my head, on top of 144 olive drab, government issue, U.S. Army comforters. I may never have fired a shot in anger (What bogey would dare risk the 69th AAA Gun Battalion's deadly fire?), but I knew an enemy that they don't show you in the recruitment posters. Now this is classified information, and I really should rip your tongue out after I divulge it. But here goes. My job was keeping the telephone lines open in case of attack. Every 30 minutes, 8 hours on, 24 hours off, from deep down inside one bunker I called up someone deep down inside another bunker and whispered, "This is Codfish. How do you read me, Defender?" and waited for the answer: "This is Defender. I read you loud and clear, Codfish!" Is your pulse racing yet? Mine neither: The enemy was boredom.

Like every GI, I made up war stories. I told friends and family I was the battalion hymnist. I told them I rose through ranks all the way from private to corporal. I said I wrote doggerel, "I have no use for the battery commander, and the first sergeant's not much grander." I claimed the coat I was issued fit *so well* it drew salutes and the cry of "Halt!" from the base MP. "Coat! Where're you going with that soldier?" I boasted that my salute was so snappy, officers would take another walk around the parade ground just to see it twice. I did respond once to the commanding general who complimented me one morning, "Ah, Corporal Lebenthal, sweeping the floor I see . . ." "Yes Sir, General," I said throwing him one of those coveted salutes, "Never too big to sweep a floor, sir."

After two years, I was out of the army and ready to do battle with the really tough nuts in Hollywood.

Loudon Wainwright in his book, *The Great American Magazine: An Inside History of Life* (Knopf, 1986) says I was "*very funny.*" "Lebenthal, a bright-eyed, intense, *very funny* young man with so much energy that he seemed at times about to ignite and lift off, roamed his entertainment beat with wonder, huge enthusiasm—and his tongue often firmly planted in cheek."

I have always tried and usually succeeded in seeing the bright side of things. That is how I managed to put on a smile with subways just missed, balsa wood models that fold like an accordion when the rubber band is wound too tight, copying machines that jam just by looking at them, and faux pas that leave me not only with the smile on my face but also with my foot sticking in my mouth.

Harry Brand, the head of publicity at Twentieth Century Fox tried to get me fired my second week in Hollywood for a typical Jim Lebenthal blurt. He had just arranged for a private screening of *The Egyptian,* a turkey starring Lana Turner, Edmund Purdom, and Zanuck's protégé, Bella Darvi (a contraction of Mr. and Mrs. Zanuck's first names, Darryl and Vivian). When the lights came up, I said, "Harry, what are we going to do? The movie's awful." Brand was lame and clutched my arm to help him make it across the room to a telephone. He got right on the phone to my boss Mary Leatherbee in New York and asked where she'd found me, and why was she siccing me on the movie industry? Mary, sensing that I was probably right, killed a six-page photo essay on *The Egyptian* that had been planned and replaced it with a page and a half on the costumes and sets. But she also issued a gentle suggestion to me: "For a month, keep your big mouth shut!" When the month was up, I opened it in time to ask the producers of upcoming *Vera Cruz,* "Who's going to play the title role?"

(Vera Cruz is a place, stupid.) Anyway they said, Denise Darcel, a French cabaret singer whose broken English typecast her in Hollywood for any number of movie parts as the native girl. So, right from my lung to my tongue (as the saying goes) I made the observation of their female lead, "Oh, in other words, nobody important." Another call to Mary in New York from a studio in Hollywood: "What are you doing to us?"

I was just warming up for more serious business one day in the nation's capital. That day would come 30 years later in a U.S. Senate hearing, when I testified for my trade organization, then named the Public Securities Association, about making retirees include their municipal bond interest in figuring the tax on their Social Security benefits. I called it "unconstitutional, improper, unfair, counter-productive." I said the Social Security tax on municipal bonds only increased the burden on our cities and towns for which local taxpayers would have to foot the bill. I said such a misguided, mischievous tax was "just a potato in the petunia patch." When I finished my Jimmy Stewart-like performance from the movie *Mr. Smith Goes to Washington,* Senator Russell Long came down from his exalted chair and thanked me personally for "one of the most entertaining afternoons he'd had in the United States Senate in 35 years."

Let's hopscotch back and forth a little bit. When I left Hollywood and was circling New York for a landing in the old hometown and my family bond business, I looked down at all those indistinguishable pinpoints of light twinkling and passing under the wing in quiet anonymity. I swore I would not let the bond business take the cheerfulness, good nature, and high spirits out of me. Because the thing I still dreaded most in life was boredom. After all, I had some of the most glamorous jobs in America: *Life,* Disney, NBC, Young & Rubicam, Ogilvy & Mather. And now I was going to spend the rest of my life in dull, dreary bonds? What a feckless worry that turned out to be. The best years of my life have been spent living with bonds in boom and bust, inflation, recession, and the highest and lowest interest rates in American history—and turning the unexpected into something downright exciting.

The Cash Cow Is Not for Hamburger

Here is a story that shows how municipal bonds combine boom and bust. Boom when you buy them. Bust after you pay for them. Only it is not as bad as it sounds.

Go back. It is back in 1994. The Federal Reserve, the nation's central bank and steward of price stability has suddenly reversed gears and raised the Federal Funds Rate, the bellwether for short-term interest rates through-out the land.

I'm looking at myself in the mirror, shaving and thinking that raising the rates means that market values go down for bonds that people already own. Only in this case, it meant a whole lot down, the worst collapse in bond prices since the Great Inflation of the late 1970s. So here, 20 years later, my clients have been getting their monthly statements showing how bad the shellacking would be if they had to sell their bonds before maturity.

So, I'm asking that lathered guy in the mirror, "Okay Lebenthal, what do you say now?" Did you ever warn your new investors that bonds go up and bonds go down? Did you ever show new recruits the investment equivalent of the VD film? Did you tell them that munis may not be an object of speculation in and of themselves, but that bond prices are inextricably tied to the tail of the 30-year Treasury bond, which is the plaything of speculators in world financial markets? In other words, what did you ever say to prepare your clients for today?

It is cold comfort that most individual investors buy to hold and don't have to sell. Because their monthly statements would quickly show that if they did have to sell, they would get their clocks cleaned, along with the big boys like George Soros. Only, the problem is they are not George Soros. And they are not billionaires with lots of financial cushions to soften the sting. Most are not millionaires. They are like John Tagliani of Tenafly, New Jersey, who wrote me in anguish that the money he had invested in municipal bonds was hard-earned savings he had scrimped for and scrupulously put aside from a salary. You see, the mainstay of the municipal bond market these days is retail, meaning the guy on the street. "Retail" buys for income, not to speculate on market moves. Moms and Pops are the real buyers of real municipal bonds, and they pay for them with their own (not borrowed) money.

I hold my nose clear of the last elusive whiskers, finish the ablutions and head downtown for the first watery gargle of the telephone ringing in despair. Someone has already received his statement. Just my luck, it is an old family friend who knew me as a boy and who had poured all his gotten gains from the sale of his girlie magazine empire into my safe, sound municipal bonds. He and I have been through the New York City Fiscal Crisis together and the great inflation. And now this—a falling-domino-like, money-losing sequence beginning with Alan Greenspan jiggering the Federal Funds rate, then hedges collapsing, speculators dumping, and the sell-off sucking everything attached to the tiger's tail into the toilet. Seymour (as I'll call him), is down 20 percent in net worth. He is fairly along in years and is a serious clinical depressive. In the army, they taught us how to take a penknife and cut a hole in the trachea of a choking buddy. I'm thinking penknife, tranquilizer gun, Heimlich maneuver, anything to address Seymour's gasping at the other end of the telephone.

Seymour! Catch your breath and repeat after me: "I didn't buy to sell! I didn't buy to sell!" It's an old mantra I have used before to cure hyperventilation in the holders of my bonds. And for Seymour, being only a generation or two removed from the old country, I've got an even more calming nostrum. "Seymour. What were your ancestors thinking when they bought the family cow? Milk, Seymour! Milk! And the good they'd get from the family cow every morning and evening at milking time. *Not* how much moo-la they'd get if they sold the cow for hamburger. *Think milk, Seymour! Milk now. Not hamburger at the end!*"

I think I've got Seymour thinking. I can hear his steady breathing again. That's good. Seymour is entering a state of bovine contentment, imagining a big, beautiful brown-eyed cash cow, gushing forth interest right along and the entire hunk of cash he was promised at maturity. I—who know better than ever to tell a depressive, "Buck up, what have you got to be depressed about?"—also know in my heart that I have given a client and old friend a reason to live, so he can cash in his bonds at maturity for everything coming to him. By my calculation, that will be when Seymour will be pushing 103. Long life, Seymour!

Quenching a City's Thirst with Saltwater

Forty years ago, New York City announced it would issue bonds to close its budget gap. I was new in the bond business and still wet behind the ears. But that didn't stop me. I hustled right up to City Hall. "Mr. Chairman, you can't do that," I told the boss of the Board of Estimate. "You can't stick future taxpayers with the debt for this year's expendables." I told him borrowing for papers, pencils, and daily operating expenses is the kiss of death. I told him that "issuing first-priority bonds to pay for expenses is obscene."

I told him: "Only as long as capital improvements add to the productive assets of the community can communities borrow without watering down their ability to pay."

I told him: "Using bonds to borrow for consumption would be like a farmer eating the seed corn, gobbling up the laying hens, and devouring the breeding bull for steaks!"

He told me, in so many words, "Get lost: We need the money. Where else are we going to get it?"

I should have said something like this: "From capital that creates more capital. Capital that creates jobs and incomes and tax revenues." But it would take years before I understood exactly what business I was in: converting people's savings into the tools of production to improve the economy for everybody.

There's a helluva difference between a bond issued to close a budget gap and a bond issued to build a subway. A new subway has a multiplier effect that adds real value to the community and also yields a payback for years to come. On the other hand, deficit financing goes up in smoke; once the money's spent, it is gone, with nothing to show for it. What you are really doing when you borrow for today's consumption is just passing on the debt (with interest) to future generations.

But that is what happened. And so, New York borrowed hand over fist to pay for the daily costs of running the town and was on its way to the fiscal crisis of 1975. City bonds would become the laughingstock of the investment world. And when that happened, "opportunity came knocking at the door," as Sayra Lebenthal put it. "The insurance companies saw a good thing, and got in on it. How? By carrying coals to Newcastle and charging to guarantee payment of municipal bonds that are essentially creditworthy to begin with."

I was on the board of directors of one such financial guarantor, MBIA. Even in my prestigious position as an MBIA director, the idea of the insurance companies of the United States guaranteeing the payment of the bonds of our great American cities and states, took something precious out of my life. Before municipal bond insurance, I could weave a thing of beauty out of the story of municipal bond safety. How tax collections were going in Broken Bow, debt outstanding in Horse Cough, any big taxpayers moving in or out of Butternuts-Unadilla, how many times user fees exceeded debt service of the Veteran's Memorial Bridge . . . whatever.

Then suddenly half the bonds we sold were insured and rated triple-A. Like those old Navajos who used to weave fancy blankets, which they now buy from JCPenney, I had no more stories to weave out of all the yarns about municipal bond safety. Insured municipal bonds made a Maytag repairman out of me. A few suspicious investors still ask, "Suppose everything goes down at once, who insures the insurers?" That's when I go into my song and dance about the insurers insuring only what is creditworthy to begin with; how to be rated triple-A, an insured bond goes through the wringer at the rating agencies; and how rating agency reserve requirements and their risk-based capital charges take the incentive out of insuring riskier bonds. Municipal bond safety just isn't the talking point it used to be, until a New York City fiscal crisis, Orange County, California, bankruptcy, or "Whoops!" happens, and the flag touches the ground.

If the Economics Aren't There, and the People Are against a Bond, "Whoops!"

The Washington Public Power Supply System (WPPSS) holds the record. And its bonds brought down on the head of the municipal bond industry the worst default in its history, for which WPPSS became known as "Whoops!" You'd call it worse than that if you were left holding the bag for $2.25 billion bonds that the court called "a mistake," "a frustration of purpose," and "an impracticality," and then repudiated any obligation to pay.

How does a $2,250,000,000 "mistake" happen?

One mistake in the Pacific Northwest of the 1970s was hyped forecasts of energy demand and groundless warnings by the region's electricity wholesaler, the dam-building, power-hungry federal Bonneville Power Administration: Hey, Washington, Oregon, Idaho! There will be no more cheap, abundant energy, unless your public utilities get together and participate in building two huge new nuclear energy plants. And those were the infamous WPPSS Projects 4 and 5.

If Project 4 and 5 bonds had been revenue bonds, pure and simple, paid solely from sales of nuclear power, default would come under the heading "inability to pay." No power sales, no revenues. But WPPSS 4 and 5 bonds were backed by a security mechanism called "take or pay." Eighty-eight municipal and investor-owned utilities in the three states jointly promised to charge local electricity customers whatever it might take to meet the costs of the projects, including debt service, come "hell or high water," no matter whether the nuclear plants ever got built.

No local utility wanted to lose a potential new factory because it couldn't provide it with enough electricity. So, to keep up with the anticipated demand for energy, the 88 utilities went out on a limb. They would sign those take-or-pay agreements for their share of any power WPPSS generated and pass on the construction costs to their own customers. That meant the utilities (and their customers)—and not the bondholders—would take on the "dry hole" risk, if the plants never produced an erg of energy. The second big mistake: not considering how ratepayers would take to higher electricity bills.

For decades, from 1938 to 1965, the cost of residential electric rates in the Pacific Northwest never went up. Even by 1971, the region still had the lowest rates in the nation. Like fresh air, clean water, and the pure, driven snow, cheap energy was considered a birthright in Washington, Oregon, and Idaho. But construction delays and huge cost overruns would soon spoil the good thing, when they started showing up on folks' electric bills. So with the Three Mile Island disaster, the fall of nuclear power from grace, and the realization that none of the plants could ever produce electricity economically, the people of the Pacific Northwest pulled the plug. "Enough already!" They told their utility companies, "Stop paying those bond holders." They argued that their 88 utilities did not have the legal authority to enter into take-or-pay contracts in the first place. And the courts in the three states backed them up. Without the consent of the people, the public utilities could not just write bondholders a blank check that was siphoning every local electricity customer's personal bank account.

On June 15, 1983, the Washington State Supreme Court declared the take-or-pay, come-hell-or-high-water participant agreements securing WPPSS Projects 4 and 5 bonds to be "invalid." This wasn't like New York City going broke and defaulting. It was repudiation of debt by elected judges in three states. It was out-and-out Refusal— Unwillingness to Pay.

By 1995—after 12 years of waiting—bondholders had received 7 or 8 cents on the dollar from whatever money WPPSS had in its bond fund, and another 30 cents on the dollar from settlement agreements making peace with security firms that had underwritten and sold the bonds and the bond attorneys who had deemed take-or-pay legal in the first place. (Amazingly, take-or-pay is legal and binding in other states and the WPPSS courts could have decided either way.)

The states of Washington, Oregon, and Idaho got out of WPPSS for the same reason the nation got out of Vietnam. People didn't like the war. People in the Northwest didn't like paying the kind of tab for electricity that we in the East take in stride. When push comes to shove, the public has to like what a bond is for: a necessity of life, a public purpose imbued with essentiality and good public policy. Public policy is how a society decides what's good, what's bad. Public policy is the altar at which politicians, the public, and the press worship. The *legal* obligation of a municipal bond to pay comes as close to the Absolute as you can get on paper. But Public Policy (Capital P, Capital P) is the pair of aces that beats a pair of kings. In the Pacific Northwest, WPPSS was Bad Public Policy. Here's my theory, and let the bond attorneys shoot me for it: when the economics aren't there and the people are against it: Whoops!

Thud! Thrown by the High Court Off My High Horse

From my star performance in the Senate Social Security tax hearing, I moved on to the next stage: breakfast speaker. I was the one booked into the first slot of the day at conferences and conventions to wake up and shake up audiences about the attackes in Congress on federalism and the imunity of our sovereign states and their bonds, under the Constitution, from federal destruction. In a word, taxation. One morning at Windows on the World, I stood in front of my trade organization. I brandished *The Man Who Mistook His Wife for a Hat* by Dr. Oliver Sacks (Simon & Schuster: Summit, New York, 1985) in one hand, and the 1,379-page *Tax Reform Act of 1986* in the other. In that legislation, 113 pages were devoted to munis and clipping the wings of their exemption from federal income taxes.

LEBENTHAL: This is the case of Doctor P, a brilliant musician who thinks his wife is a hat and vice versa. So Doctor Sacks makes a house call on Doctor P, and he writes this: "I had stopped at a florist on my way to his apartment, and bought myself an extravagant red rose for my buttonhole. Now I removed this and handed it to him. 'Smell it,' I suggested. And he looked somewhat puzzled, as if I had asked him to smell a higher symmetry. He complied courteously, and he took it to his nose. Now suddenly he came to life. He beautifully exclaimed: 'Ah! An early rose, what a heavenly smell!' He started to hum Die Rose, Die Lilie. His reality, it seemed, could be conveyed by smell, but not by sight."

I put Dr. Sacks down and then lifting the Tax Act to my nose, theatrically breathed in once, then twice and pronounced, "This is no rose!"

If that was the first laugh that the bond business brass got out of the Tax Reform Act of 1986, it was also the last. The 1986 Act had prohibited the issuance of certain tax-frees outright. It subjected certain others to volume caps. It limited the types of bonds banks could buy and still deduct their cost of carry. It limited how many times a bond could be refunded and still qualify for tax exemption. It required municipal issuers to rebate to Uncle Sam earnings on bond proceeds temporarily invested in construction funds and debt reserve funds. It created the alternative minimum tax on so-called private activity bonds.

A little history: Ever since the first income tax act in 1913, the aroma of tax-free municipal bonds had wafted under Treasury's nose like apple pie cooling on the windowsill. Just as in the old movies when a hobo or Pluto the Pup tried to pinch the pie, the federal government—with gaping deficits to close in the early 1980s—became the pup and eyed that pie just watering at the mouth.

I am not a lawyer. I barely passed Constitutional Law at Princeton. But you didn't have to clerk for Oliver Wendell Holmes to see that using municipal bond interest as one part of gross income to get at another part of gross income, like Social Security benefits, was a tax on the bonds themselves. So Lebenthal & Company bankrolled *Boli v. Baker* (putting our dough behind

Mary and Louis Boli versus Treasury Secretary James Baker) to have the Social Security Tax on municipal bonds declared unconstitutional.

Our side argued, "but for having to throw their bond income into the pot, Mr. and Mrs. Boli would not have had any tax to pay on their Social Security benefits." Using munibond interest to get at their benefits was tantamount to a tax on their munis. Our theory was if it walks like a duck, quacks like a duck, it is a duck.

Two levels of the judicial system disagreed. It is not a duck. It is a measurement. And the court hinted, even if it were a tax on the Boli's municipal bonds, don't press the point. The day of any constitutional basis for exempting state and local bonds from federal taxation was fast fading. In fact, when I stepped onto the ground at Phoenix Sky Harbor International Airport in May 1988, it had faded.

Every income tax code since 1913 had spelled out a provision for the exemption of state and local bonds from federal taxation. Congress had always affirmed legislatively what was accepted constitutional doctrine—that under the Reserved Powers clause of the Tenth Amendment, neither the states nor the federal government could tax the bonds of the other. But then in *South Carolina v. Baker,* the Supreme Court took the argument for tax exemption off its constitutional high horse and placed its protection squarely in the hands of Congress. Said the Court, "States must find their protection from Congressional regulation through the national political process." That meant mustering the votes in Congress to keep municipal bonds tax free.

I was in Phoenix on my way to make another rousing speech on my pet theme: reciprocal tax immunity under the Tenth Amendment, my "tax exemption here, now, and forever" speech. As I stepped off the plane, I heard my name on the airport PA system and got a message to call my office: Better give a different speech, Jim. The decision of the court has killed your old one about the Constitution, dead! So there I was, a walking encyclopedia on now out-moded case law, with only one hour until showtime to adapt to the new law and change my tune.

"Nothing's changed folks," I told my audience of issuers from the Salt River Project and the municipal bond dealers who underwrote their tax-free bonds. "Your bonds are still free of federal income tax. The only difference now is that tax exemption is a gift from Congress, to give or take away. For 20 years, Congress has been acting that way anyway. Only now it's official. Putting tax exemption in the hands of the 'political process,' was telling us one thing. No matter where a right comes from, its survival depends on someone standing up and fighting for it."

You know me. I love a good fight. Furthermore, I had a personal reason to stand up and stick a neck out to keep the federal government's hands off my babies: the verity I had learned at my mother's knee, "Municipal bonds are safe and sound, Son, and *tax-free!* Now and forever!"

I spit on my hands, puffed out my chest, and threw down the gauntlet. I would get political. I would imbue municipal bonds with what WPPSS lacked: essentiality, good public purpose, "good public policy." I would ro-mance the infrastructure, running commercials on great public works. My rallying cry? "Built by Bonds." I would get up there on radio and TV and rename myself, Jim "Built by Bonds" Lebenthal. For someone who had thought municipal bonds were going to be dishwater dull, I was embarked on a rip-roaring good time.

LEBENTHAL TO GO

Ever notice how all groups
are alike, made up of leaders,
followers, troupers, and party poopers?
Don't like your niche?
Change your stripes.

Floating bonds to cure the
deficit in like quenching a
thown's thirst with saltwater.
You're just making it worse.

So how do you know a bond is
any good before you buy it?
Did the people vote for it?
Is the project up and running?
Is it so needed there's not only
the legal obligation to pay,
but a commonsense one.

Boli v. Baker . . . Brown v. Board
of Education . . . Roe v. Wade
It's surprising what can
happen when an ordinary
citizen gives a damn.

No matter where a right comes
from, its survival depends
on someone screaming
bloody murder, standing up,
fighting—even singing—for it.

7

"Don't Do It," Said the Birds

No Lying, Cheating, Stealing. It Is Not Allowed.

Remember the movie *Brigadoon?* It opens with a scene at the bar of the "21" Club in New York City. To establish New York as a place to get out of and set the mood for finding paradise in Brigadoon, the camera pans along a row of Madison Avenue types at the bar and unforgettably overhears one of them confessing, "I'll lie for that company. I'll cheat. And I'll steal. But I will not sacrifice my integrity." Don't you love that quote? I do, because it also sets the stage for drama in the bond business, where a wrong may be legal, but it sure isn't right.

I'm not talking about high-profile lowlifes like Ebbers, Lay, Rigas the father, Rigas the son, or even Kozlowski, whose names you already know. What worries me professionally is that today's culture of success at any price has everybody doing 70 in the 55 mph zone just to keep up with the traffic. (Myself included. I just got a ticket on the Taconic Parkway for doing 80. So make sure you slow down around Milan, New York.)

What I hate is when a broker says he is passing on a bargain to you that is dirt cheap. Why? Because somebody else had to sell. Well, at least he's putting you on notice, "Don't call us, if you have to sell. Because we're going to screw you, too."

I hate it when somebody offers a 6 percent two-year bond at, say, 106 and tells you only how great the current yield is: 5.66 percent! Sure it is great, but the truth will out in two years, when you cash in that bond and get back just its face value. Between cashing the coupons right along and the bond itself at maturity, you're going to wind up with just its actual yield to maturity: 2.88 percent.

I hate it when a broker says he's got a great buy, rated "A," and doesn't tell you it was recently downgraded a whole notch from "Aa." An "A" that has just been upgraded from "Baa" beats an "A" that's just been downgraded from "Aa."

Like Groucho said to the woman on *You Bet Your Life* who coyly admitted her age as "approaching 60." "Oh? From which direction?"

I hate tax swaps that are not fairly presented, where it looks as if you are getting out of one bond and into another, without having to put up a cent, but also getting money back. Who is kidding whom? You are paying both the getting-out cost of the one bond and the getting-in cost of the other. They're hidden . . . in the commensurately lesser market value of the new bond you are swapping into.

I hate it when I am tarred by someone else's fast talk, half-truths, sins of omission as well as commission, in short somebody else's doing "bad business."

Once upon a time, this municipal bond business was a fraternity of hidebound, duty-bound professionals. A visit to a municipal bond house at the height of the trading day was like a museum scene by Madame Tussaud . . . or a movie of the Supreme Court in its sleep at night. Virtue, innocence, and dignity not marred even by the sound of heavy breathing. Then, following the astronomical interest rates of 1969 to 1970, and the ensuing feeding frenzy for yields of 7 percent and more—tax-free!—a new species of municipal bond man crawled out of the sea: the "Bond Daddies." Preying on the clueless greenhorns who had never given municipal bonds so much as a nod in passing, the Bond Daddies hastened the day the SEC and its policing arm, the National Association of Securities Dealers (NASD) cracked down on the once oh, so gentlemanly municipal bond industry.

Where does my own sense of right and wrong still come from? The penal code? Fear of a mother's scolding? I'm convinced it is the nattering of a "Don't-Do-It Bird" in my conscience, just like the birds in the story of *Nutcracker and Sugar Dolly* that my German *Fräulein* would read to me in her thick accent, telling Nutcracker and Sugar Dolly not to go into the woods. "Don't do it, Nutcracker! Don't do it, Sugar Dolly, Don't you do it either, Jim. Stay out of the woods."

"Don't You Pay to Play, Jim!"

I am always taken aback when a company's code of ethics has to say that no lying, cheating, or stealing is allowed. I always thought that kind of thing was illegal anyway, like slipping money under the table to a local official to throw the town's underwriting business your way. What's happened to us that we need a rule specifically telling us bribery's illegal? Arthur Levitt Jr., as Chairman of the Securities and Exchange Commission (SEC) obviously felt that we munibond fellows did. And he made donating more than $250 to any state or local politician who could award underwriting business punishable by two years' expulsion from underwriting that municipality's bonds. And before you could give even the $250, you had to be eligible to vote for that politician.

I used to give money to politicians: $1,000 here; $1,000 there. And I did it because I expected something in return, but I'll bet it is not what you think. I wanted the candidates to know me and my cause: the preservation of tax exemption. I wanted them to fight for their ability to borrow on the cheap so they could finish building this country with low-cost tax-free municipal bonds. Infrastructure is usually the last thing on a candidate's mind, so I wrote those checks even to candidates I couldn't vote for.

I gave to Republicans. I gave to Democrats. Before I sent the check, I sometimes asked a candidate to read over my speeches on the contribution of public investment to higher standards of living and call me back with comments. (I usually gave whether they called or not.) In one speech, I itemized, one by one, the checks I had written out to politicians totaling $12,375 that year and explained my motive for each. I confessed I was seeking the allocation of a scarce resource to public works . . . that I was patently out to influence how people, including their leaders, feel about incurring debt for productive investment.

Finally, I hated the infringement of my right to support someone running for office who shared my ideals. So, I fought the good fight against the rule banning political contributions right up to the final day for registering objections with the SEC. And then I gave up. I wrote Chairman Levitt that I was making my peace with G-37, the rule in question, and would forever hold my tongue, because "severing the tie between political contributions and the award of business was unimpeachable." Luckily, I had an alternative for influencing public opinion. I would just keep running those Lebenthal commercials, "Love My Sewer, Love My Bonds," "Love my Subway, Love My Bonds," "Love My Towers, Love My Bonds." I'd keep my integrity intact and sell my munibonds at the same time.

"And Don't Feed Any More Birds, Jim"

We've all suffered our share of blunders and terrible accidents from not heeding the warning of the Don't-Do-It Bird. For example, one of my misdeeds actually involved little birds themselves, and I am mortified by it to this day.

When I reached the age of reason, seven, I decided to feed the baby birds inside their birdhouse in Aunt Bessie's backyard in Red Bank, New Jersey. First I attached an earthworm onto the notch of a clothes pole and gingerly poked it into the opening of the bird house. Poking again, I accidentally knocked the birdhouse down. The doomed chicks fell out, wiggling and fluttering around my feet. I panicked and did a terrible thing. I stomped on them and tried to get rid of the evidence. But when Aunt Bessie came home, she saw right away what I had done. She was apoplectic. And I had no heart for even trying to explain. What was my defense? Pure stupidity? I couldn't admit cruelty to animals. I just hung my head in shame. Why didn't the birds speak up? "Don't do it, Jim. We're not hungry. Please don't feed us any more."

Recently, I asked my 11-year-old grandson, Ben, if he would play me and reenact the birdhouse scene for a movie on my life. He said, "No! Please don't make me play you."

I asked Ben, "Why not?"

"Because I don't want to wear your business suit."

"Don't Feed Another Derivative to Citron, Jim"

"Who or what is Citron," you ask? *Sic transit gloria!*

Robert Citron was the reckless treasurer of Orange County, California, who bankrupted his county playing the derivatives market.

Derivatives are Wall Street's newest atomic weapon. They can be a hedge against losses. But derivatives can also blow up and go nuclear. And losses, compounding on losses, can wipe out a county and (sorry about that, Orange County) did. Of course, as the National Rifle Association always says: "Guns don't kill, people do." Well, that means derivatives are only as good as the hand that wields them. And Citron was wielding them wildly, doubling and tripling his bets in derivatives to cover losses that were compounding—and we know from the racetrack, "Scared money never wins!" The inevitable time came when Orange County had to file for bankruptcy. Selling derivatives to Citron had all the benefits to society of plying a drunk with boilermakers. But while Citron was deservedly crucified in the press, you didn't hear much breast-beating from Wall Street about its own role in violating the suitability rule and bringing the walls of the temple down on the head of the whole industry.

I could not have felt worse if those were bonds that I had sold now being plunged into default and dragged through the mud. In a rare angry Lebenthal newsletter, I chewed out not only Citron, but all of Wall Street. I asked my colleagues, "Quick! Answer," "Am I my brother's keeper?" I thought I could hear their wheels turning: "Let me think, let me think. Am I my brother's keeper?" Well, dammit. At Lebenthal, I want the answer to be an instant "yes," without even having to think about it.

"Don't Be a Dim Bulb, Jim"

I hate dim bulbs in high places.

A dim bulb lets the generator run out of gasoline.

A dim bulb can't see the difference between borrowing for paper, pencils, salaries, and expendables and borrowing for an electric generating plant (that also generates the revenues to pay for the necessities of life).

A dim bulb saddles taxpayers with $5 billion in debt service over the next 30 years (with nothing to show for the money) to save $2 billion over the next four years on bonds that were just getting around to maturing. But that is exactly what Mayor Bloomberg did awhile back when he refinanced the remaining MAC bonds to close a gap in New York City's current operating budget. For all the money, he got no new schools, no new bridges, no new waterworks, no new power plants.

One fine day, a dim bulb lets the United States go dark from the East Coast to Cleveland. Where were you in the Big Blackout of 2003? I was deep underground in a New York City subway with my daughter Alexandra, when the train groaned to a dead stop. I wanted to blame what was happening on an exogenous force, or on a cluck like Homer Simpson perhaps having dropped a monkey wrench into the electric works, or even a terrorist, for god's sake. I mean, external enemies we can deal with. National incompetence is something else. So, climbing out of the car down onto the tracks, into the darkness, through the tunnel, and at last out and up to the street at Grand Central Station, Alexandra and I were faced by the accusing finger of daylight and an Awful Truth: Let's face it, once again, as in 1965 and 1977, the Blackout of 2003 happened because of dim bulbs in high places: the failure of the United States to provide the generators, the transmission lines, the grid, the nuts and bolts for the nation's energy needs. Dem bulbs, dem bulbs, dem dim bulbs. Oh, hear the word of the birds.

"Don't Go off Half-Cocked, Jim"

Mistakes happen. Here's a snafu, 100 percent man-made and ridiculously costly. This beaut happened when I worked in Hollywood. The script of *Strategic Air Command* called for an air rescue by helicopter in Thule, Greenland. Paramount Pictures decided with typical Hollywood-think that it would be more practical to build the set on its largest soundstage, blanket the floor with 500 tons of artificial snow, and fly a real helicopter indoors.

The pilot started his rotor. Then the special effects men fired up the three wind machines, and in an instant, the stage was a maelstrom of an angry Nordic blizzard, and the blades were doing 1700 RPM, just short of takeoff speed! Invisible currents were clawing clumsily at the walls when the fake realism of Thule was rent by 148 feet of canvas sky splitting along its horizon line. In the turbulent downdraft, lights shook, patches of floor were blown bare, sky backing began rippling like a lake, and a rip had darted like a nylon run along a seam near the bottom of the backing. The thrill of blazing air trails indoors was delayed

2½ hours. A stagehand was heard to mutter, "All they had to do was tell the Air Force they wanted to shoot in Thule, and they'd have been flown there like that."

I recall a different snafu that was 100 percent my fault for trying to micromanage something I knew nothing about: office maintenance and cleaning. At Lebenthal, night after night, pairs of ratty old high-heeled shoes covered the floor of the office closet where I hung my coat. In a well-run office, dammit, they'd be out the window or in a Goodwill Industries bin in a trice, I thought. But it took me a long while to act on that thought, and the shoes piled up just like those old magazines at home. Finally, one night, I gave those shoes the axe. Out they went, every one of them, into the dumpster and down the freight elevator in the back. Mission accomplished. Fade out. Fade in.

A little while later at Lebenthal & Company, we had to fire a kleptomaniac. Everybody in the office was talking about different stuff that had gone missing. Then somebody said, "I wonder if it was that same sicko who stole all the women's shoes." My solar plexus plexed. I guess my red cheeks, dropping jaw, and the smack of my own palm on my own forehead gave me away. It hadn't occurred to me that all of our Wall Street women who wore sneakers on the subway kicked off their office dress shoes at 5 P.M. and left them in a closet every night. That's why, after I had thrown out all those Manolo Blahniks, our Lebenthal ladies started wearing their walk-to-work sneakers during office hours. Betrayed by my blush, I said, "Treat's on me, ladies. Ice cream sodas for everybody. And I'll take crow for myself."

"Don't Wave Flags, Jim"

I'll never forget the day that Lebenthal stuck its neck way out for New York City. We ran a full-page ad that boldly called general obligation bonds (GOs), like those of New York City, "The Second Safest Investment in America," I got two utterly different telephone calls. One was from Mayor Abe Beame, saying, "Thank you, Mr. Lebenthal." The other was from the Public Securities Association, saying, "Lebenthal, you better get yourself a good lawyer." Even though municipal bond advertising was not subject to the same stringent rules and regulations that applied to stocks, munis sure weren't exempt from Section 10b-5, the provision in securities law that commands, "Don't mislead the public." We didn't get a lawyer. We got a bevy of them. Eventually, the substance of the ad was vindicated, but not the tone. The SEC's investigation into the sales of New York City bonds found all the flag waving for New York City to be overblown, misleading, and unbecoming of a securities professional.

Over the years, Lebenthal's colorful and most unbanker-like advertising must have been taunting the regulators . . . in fact, it had them licking their chops, panting for the day we would come under their purview. That day came with a bang when we began marketing bond funds. A fund of municipal bonds is different from an individual municipal bond. A fund is an "investment company." And investment company advertising must be cleared by the SEC's enforcement arm, the National Association of Securities Dealers (NASD). I was ready to comply. They were ready to pounce.

In late 1995, the NASD called me on the carpet for making an exaggerated claim about our Empire Builder Municipal Bond Fund. Here's my heinous headline, "All we did was lasso the moon." The reference was from *It's a Wonderful Life,* the Christmas perennial starring Jimmy Stewart. But the regulators took the headline literally. (Incidentally, the rest of the ad noted that for four months our fund had turned in a higher total return than 75 rival funds and that while we didn't promise the moon, we did make some customers' dreams come a little closer and quicker with our Empire Builder.)

Another ad that curled the overseers' hair showed Alexandra first as 14-year-old girl and then as the grown-up president of Lebenthal & Company, under this headline: "Because you can't believe how fast the last 20 years went by is why you should plan for the next 20 now." This time I got my creative knuckles rapped for promising everlasting success and using (can you believe it?) inappropriate language.

The overseers objected to my use of *wondrous* as innocuously as this: "By reinvesting your dividends in additional fund shares every month, something *wondrous* will happen. No matter what interest rates do, or how share price fluctuates, the number of shares you own will always be growing, building and rebuilding on itself in good markets and bad." I acknowledged that share value down the road could be lower (or higher) than its original cost. So how you would fare when you redeemed your shares would depend on the price of shares then (times the number of shares you owned). But I argued that the more shares you accumulated through reinvestment, the bigger

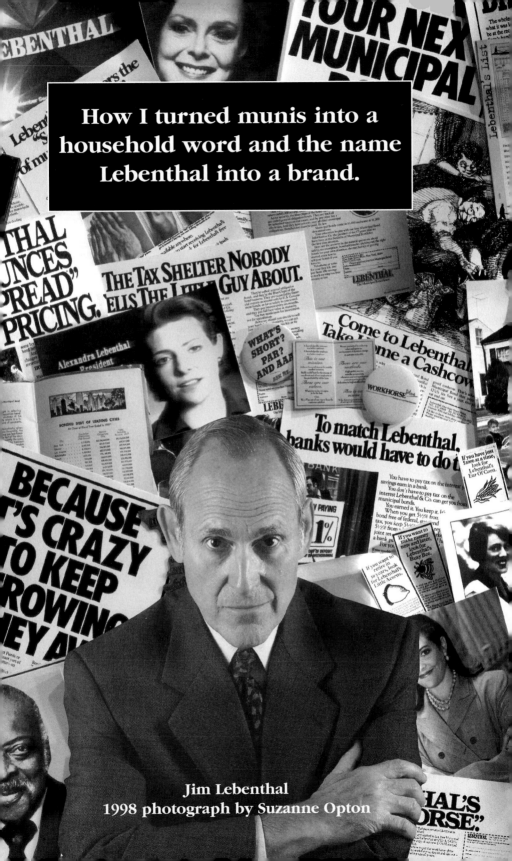

How I turned munis into a household word and the name Lebenthal into a brand.

Jim Lebenthal
1998 photograph by Suzanne Opton

I had two parents, with two used desks, and a big idea:

Sayra Fischer (b. 1898) met Louis S. Lebenthal (b. 1899), while cramming for the bar exam. They married in March 1925. Six months later they started Lebenthal & Co. on a shoestring. They rejected the one reply to their ad for capital from a "four flusher trying to distribute stocks in his public utility company." What was the utility?

Municipal bonds! (For the little guy.)

"Two telephone poles and one wire," said Mother, slightly exaggerating. Sayra Lebenthal wasn't fazed by being a pioneer woman in business. "I had a brain, an education, and a law degree (Syracuse, class of 1920)," she said. "Why not put partners in marriage to work as partners in business? It was strictly fifty-fifty. Same hours, same pay."

Mom and Dad ran ads and spoke up.

Lebenthal Sees Gain

Holds Hoover Plan Will Aid Municipal Financing

Municipal financing machinery
the country will be immediately affect
by the proposed Hoover bank pool pl
and an early return to conditions a
proximating normal may be antic
pated when the plan is put into effe
in the opinion of Louis S. Lebenth
head of Leben~~thal & Co~~

"Municipal i

LEBENTHAL HAIL
RISING BOND

In Review of Munici
Market He Cites High Marks

The average bond prices of eleven
first-grade cities and of twenty
large
new

This Is No Time
To Let Go Of
MUNICIPAL BONDS

When continued pressure by certain brokers
is being brought to bear on investors in municipal securities to have them exchange
their securities for those of other municipalities, it is fitting that this phase of the municipal bond situation be clarified.

To be a clearinghouse for all those $1,000 odd lots, Lebenthal & Co. had to get famou
So Dad fed the press forecasts and annual reviews on munis, calming markets durin
the Depression. The *ABC of Municipal Bonds,* by Louis S. Lebenthal (Harper
Brothers, 1937), nailed down his reputation as the voice of the bond busines

They became famous.

JANUARY, 1929

SMART SET
The Young Woman's Magazine

VOLUME 83,
NUMBER 5

Photograph by Hal Phyfe

THE BROKER

Yes, Sir, That's My Baby!

BLACKSTONE? BAH!—Court work fine, says Mrs. Lebenthal, woman lawyer, but there's no court could interfere with her care for daughter, and she would wel-

WEDNESDAY MORNING, NOVEMBER 24, 1926

The Firm of Lebenthal & Co.

door of room 1602, Equitable Building, there
the following legend: "Lebenthal & Co., Spe-
Odd Lot Municipal Bonds, L. S. Lebenthal,
enthal." The casual observer, if he thinks
matter at all, naturally infers that the Leben-
brothers or father and son. Such is not the
ver. Louis S. and Sayra F. Lebenthal are
a marriage, as well as in the odd-lot bond

as is known, this firm is the only one in the
which husband and wife are the sole partners.
marital standpoint, this firm started in March

his business career in a lawyer's office. Following this
he was one of the organizers of Stephens & Co., of whi
he was a member for three years. Mrs. Lebenthal wa
admitted to the bar in 1923 and then became associat
with the legal firm of Miller & Wessel. Three year
later she started practicing independently.

Both Mr. and Mrs. Lebenthal firmly believe in th
advantages of a husband-and-wife partnership. Mr
Lebenthal declares that unlike some partners, a marrie
couple are both whole-heartedly interested in their join
success and this fact is bound to make them work harde

H. L. Mencken's *Smart Set* magazine crowned Mom the "prettiest lady broker," and simply giving birth to my sister Eleanor in 1927 made the financial pages. "Sexist," would not enter the language for many years, by which time Sayra had found her forte: selling.

I grew up with munis, but I was out to see it all.

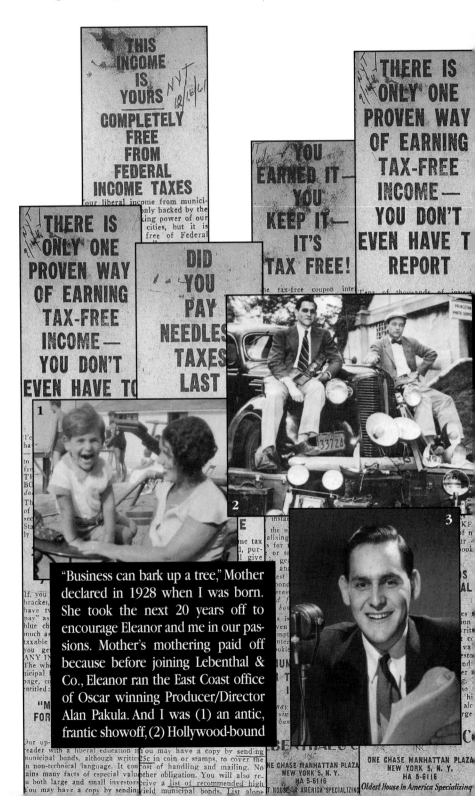

THIS INCOME IS YOURS COMPLETELY FREE FROM FEDERAL INCOME TAXES

THERE IS ONLY ONE PROVEN WAY OF EARNING TAX-FREE INCOME — YOU DON'T EVEN HAVE T REPORT

THERE IS ONLY ONE PROVEN WAY OF EARNING TAX-FREE INCOME — YOU DON'T EVEN HAVE T

YOU EARNED IT — YOU KEEP IT — IT'S TAX FREE!

DID YOU PAY NEEDLES TAXES LAST

"Business can bark up a tree," Mother declared in 1928 when I was born. She took the next 20 years off to encourage Eleanor and me in our passions. Mother's mothering paid off because before joining Lebenthal & Co., Eleanor ran the East Coast office of Oscar winning Producer/Director Alan Pakula. And I was (1) an antic, frantic showoff, (2) Hollywood-bound

And turn it all into art. Even a tumbleweed.

co-founder with classmate Chick Gallagher of the Princeton Photo Service, (3) first to submit his senior thesis on wire (recorded while I covered the 1948 Republican Convention), (4) Hollywood correspondent for *Life* magazine and producer of *Flash The Teenage Otter* for Walt Disney, (5) Oscar nominee for my short subject *T Is For Tumbleweed,* and (6) client, then husband, of my interior decorator, Jacqueline Beymer of Twin Falls, Idaho.

"Hello Mom, I'm coming to work! At Lebenthal."

When, at the age 35, I finally made the call, "Mom, I'm going to do for Lebenthal & Co. what I've been doing to make other companies famous." She said (after years of holding her tongue), "Good! You've got all that nonsense out of your system!"

Photograph by Yale Joel

My Mother, my Teacher, my Boss.

I never did get "all that non-sense out of my system." After learning the basics at Mother's knee, I used it to turn the most un-understood investment in America into graphic "Aha! Moments," with vivid images that made munis come alive for the masses.

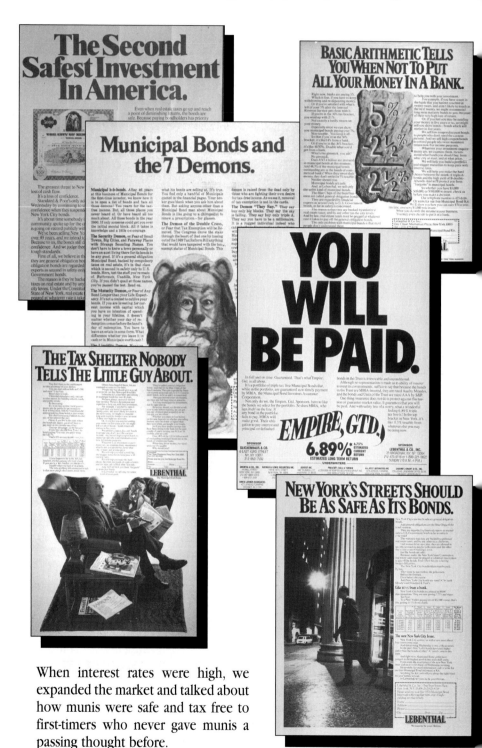

When interest rates were high, we expanded the market and talked about how munis were safe and tax free to first-timers who never gave munis a passing thought before.

(2) Why buy municipal bonds from Lebenthal?

When opportunity knocked or rates fell, to increase share of a shrinking market, we distinguished ourselves from the competition with ads about (1) Price. (2) Rescuing NYC noteholders from the Moratorium. (3) Our markups on bond sales. (4) How we go the extra mile. (5) Treating customers (like Count Basie) like one of the family.

I turned munis into Lebenthal's Workhorse, Lebenthal's

Television was the ultimate assault on the senses. Sight and sound, words and music turned munis into a household word, and Lebenthal into a brand. My favorite TV spots: (1) Love my towers, love my bonds. (2) We believe in America's Workhorse.

Cash cow, and "Lebenthal's Babies" on television.

(3) Put a little moo-la in your portfolio. (4) I'm Jim Lebenthal getting a charge from power plants "Built by Bonds." (5) I see great public works down here. (6) Love my subway, love my bonds. (7) I'm Jim Lebenthal. Municipal bonds are "My Babies."

And, like Mom and Dad, I defended "my own."

Here I am in 1983 trying to convince a Senate committee that including munibond interest in the tax on Social Security benefits is a tax on the bonds themselves. Score one for me: The Senate repealed the tax. The House and Senate in conference, however, put the tax back in. I had stuck my neck out. That's what necks are for.

And I couldn't wait to pass the torch to Alexandra.

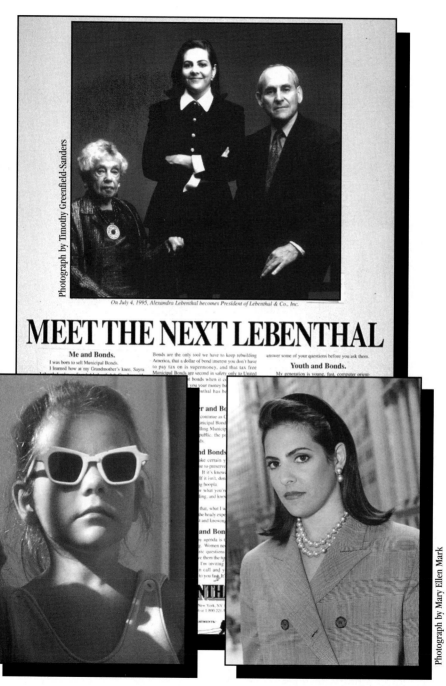

Photograph by Timothy Greenfield-Sanders

On July 4, 1995, Alexandra Lebenthal becomes President of Lebenthal & Co., Inc.

MEET THE NEXT LEBENTHAL

Me and Bonds.
I was born to sell Municipal Bonds.
I learned how at my Grandmother's knee, Sayra

Bonds are the only tool we have to keep rebuilding America, that a dollar of bond interest you don't have to pay tax on is supermoney, and that tax free Municipal Bonds are second in safety only to United t bonds when it c you your money b nthal has be

Youth and Bonds.
My generation is young, fast, computer orient-

answer some of your questions before you ask them.

r and Bc
continue as (
nicipal Bond
ling Municip
ublic. the pi
ds.

d Bonds
ake certain y
e to preserve
If it's know
If it isn't, do
g hoopla
w what you're
ling, and kno

that, what I c
he heady expe
d and knowin

and Bon
y agenda is t
Women ne
sic questions
e them the ty
I'm inviting
n call and
to you fast, b

NTH
New York, NY
at 1-800-221-

TMENTS

Photograph by Mary Ellen Mark

urprised at how fast the last 30 years went by? Then plan the next 30 now. Now that errill Lynch owns Lebenthal and doesn't intend to use the Lebenthal family name, exandra has plenty to plan herself: namely the future of the Lebenthal brand.

Go, Girl! Daddy's behind you.

Alexandra Lebenthal
2002, photograph by Luke Lois

the multiplier that would be working for you when you finally sold them.

When the NASD demanded that I delete the offending word, my legal team replied that according to the dictionary, wondrous meant "striking," and was designed to highlight that reinvestment of dividends benefits investors by increasing their number of shares in the fund. A month later, the regulators were still unbudged. "The use of the word 'wondrous' appears to exaggerate the level of growth in shares that investors will experience in the fund." And they thought my arguments to validate the use of terminology off the mark, "exaggerated and overheated in a way that confuses the accumulation of shares with investment performance. The suggestion," they argued, "was predetermining an ever successful investment—and that portraying reinvesting dividends as unique, miraculous, striking or wondrous is false."

That did it. Pushed to my limits, my legal team and I headed to Washington, the nation's capital, to personally duke it out with the NASD. But although my blood was boiling, I was Dead on Arrival.

Not long before my ill-fated mission, I had written a Lebenthal newsletter to dramatize randomness and make the unpredictability of interest rates vivid. I placed a mirror on a graph of our fund's past performance zigzagging all over the place. Lo and behold, there in the Looking Glass you could see unpredictability randomly zigzagging crazily 10 years into the future (of course, in an exact mirror image of the past). When my lawyer and I walked into a room of naysayers, all pursed lips and flared nostrils, there was enough ice in the air to freeze over Death Valley.

Had I never heard that "past performance is no guarantee of future results?" Of course I had. I was just trying to illustrate the certainty of uncertainty. "Lebenthal," the tone of the meeting unmistakably reminded me, "you're not a freshman at prep school any more depicting the rosy side of Hansen's disease in a leper colony. You're now a banker, and should be a soldier in the fight against inaccuracy, misleading exaggeration, unsupportable superlatives, cockeyed optimism."

Disclaimers, the grim regulators grimly reminded me, weren't meant to undo something you've said in an ad. They're meant to keep you from saying it. Fine with me.

I know past performance *is* no guarantee of future results. I've often said so. And I've often added, "There can be no guarantee that the fund will achieve its objectives." True enough. But can't I just tag on, "No guarantee. Just a fighting chance?" I hate it when that Don't-Do-It Bird chimes in, "No! Don't do it. Don't disclaim your own disclaimer, Jim." and kills a perfect punch line of mine.

No buts! Never, but never follow a mandated disclaimer with "Yes, but. . . ." "But" undoes every brownie point it follows, and you know it darn well.

"Don't Say 'Hate' so Much, Jim"

I'm a lover. I hate saying hate. It all goes back to the job I took after I left *Life* magazine. It was on a late-night TV show called *Tonight: America After Dark.* The program was anchored by some notorious newspaper gossip columnists assisted behind the scene by reporters whose job was to sniff out dirt for them. I, the recently very grand Hollywood correspondent for *Life,* was one of those dogged sniffers. Helen Winston was another. Helen was an aggressive go-getter, who (good grief!) had once shaved her head for a walk-on part in a women's prison movie and had been a checkout girl for Ralph's Supermarket (heavens!) in Hollywood. Helen's hair had grown back, but little things about Helen ate at me. Like the idea of Helen bald, and the idea of Helen calling her story on the retirement of the veteran ballerina, Alicia Markova, "putting the old horse out to pasture." Helen had nothing personal against me. It was I who had the problem—with Helen, the show, and, for that matter, tabloid video journalism. Within a month, I had quit *America After Dark.* But not before Helen made me take her to the premiere of the show.

I say, "Helen made me." It's more likely she said, "Gee, Jim, wanna go together?" Anyway, when I got to her place, she yelled from the shower, "I know you don't like me, but I'll bet before it's over we end up in the sack." I was too smart for that kind of gambit and sat there with my hands in my lap savoring disdain for girls who shave their heads and put great but aging ballerinas out to pasture, as if they were just old horses. Years later, I saw in the newspapers that the same Helen Winston had produced a children's movie, *Hand in Hand,* that even Eleanor Roosevelt had plugged as

117

"sensitive and adoring." And then, more years later, I read that Helen Winston had died from cancer. I recently "Googled" Helen Winston, and up she came with shaved head (before and after) and an entry about her long-lasting battle with cancer that read, "not a day in her life was without pain." There was no need to read any further. It suddenly occurred to me that I had been an additional cross for her to bear. I felt awful. I suddenly understood why hating says more about the hater than the hated.

LEBENTHAL TO GO

Whenever you find yourself
asking, "Who'll ever know?"
the answer is always the same:
"You'll know!"

If you can't find a
Don't-Do-It Bird in your local
pet shop, never fear.
You already own one—
your conscience.

Building and rebuilding the
infrastructure is how civilized societies
show they've got a future.

"Don't Do It," Said the Birds

Because there are laws,
and there are ethics,
God gave us two brains.
The left side for: Is it legal?
The right side for: Is it right?
Which are you going to listen to?

8

Lebenthal.
You Know the Name

Yours for Life
Doesn't Mean It Is Free

The coming of the dawn and the realization that you have turned your company into a "Brand" is like being shaken in your bed by a committee of Tibetans. "Hello, Dali, get up. You're the new Dali Lama."

Branding: That means your name all by itself conjures up your good points. It can make one of two identical beers taste better and one of two similar aspirins work better. In Lebenthal's case, branding is a culmination that followed 80 years of sunrise, sunset, $1.5 million a year spent on advertising, $2.5 billion worth of bonds per year sold. But converting all that mass into what people think of you, their feelings at the mention of your name, the feedback of your own reputation on what you do next, is strictly the stuff of $E = MC^2$, in which C stands for taking care of people:

Listening to them.

Answering their questions.

Making sure they understand.

Following through.

Keeping them informed.

Earning their confidence and even being a pleasure to do business with.

And doing all this to help them decide, "Yes . . . or No."

Under Generally Accepted Accounting Principles (GAAP), the market value of your company (over and above its book value) has to be reviewed and accounted for every year.

But the qualities that make you a "Brand," Aha! That's something else. Your Brand is priceless and hard to explain. Like its value to me when Jacqueline Kennedy Onassis, on a receiving line, quoted from our ad campaign and instead of saying "Nice to meet you!" introduced herself to me with, "I'm Jackie Lebenthal, one of the family."

Alexandra, a real-life Lebenthal, says that nothing makes her scratch her head more than when clients thank her for taking time to help because (they say) they know she has better things to do. "What else could I possibly have to do that's more important?"

Branding a product transforms its name into a priceless part of that product. (For all I know it may even have redemption value at the Pearly Gates.)

This chapter is about advertising, the part of branding that sears our name and its benefits into people's brains through what we say in the media. The next chapter is about what we do to live up to our brand in real life. Which is the chicken? Which is the egg? Well, that's why it takes two chapters. Please read on.

Got Bonds?

When I joined the family bond business in 1962, for most Americans there was no question as to what to do with their money. "Savings belong in a bank." At that time, "day of deposit, day of withdrawal," represented the height of most people's financial sophistication. I was determined to make municipal bonds the newest must-have creation for the masses, like margarine and frozen TV dinners.

Think of it. At that time, the Federal Reserve prohibited banks from paying more than 3¾ and then 4 percent (taxable) on deposits, and with munis paying 5 percent . . . 5½ percent . . . 6½ percent (tax-free!), why you could be in a zero tax bracket, on home relief, and still belong in munis. Back then, for a married couple filing a joint return on $35,000 annual income in New York City, getting 6 percent triple tax exempt from the bond of any municipality issued in New York State was like getting 12 percent from a bank. That is what is known as a captive consumer market, worthy of trying to crack.

So I exploited the same showmanship and skills I used on Madison Avenue to sell everything from technology to dog food, to demystify what I called the most "ununderstood" investment in America. The canvas I used to paint my bold strokes was advertising.

122

At Lebenthal, we are in a perpetual battle for people's minds. And the way to the mind is not always rational. The Duke of Windsor titled his autobiography *The Heart Has Its Reasons.* I am here to tell you that the "Mind Has Its Passions" and my mind loves advertising agencies. I mean, my mother told me to drink my milk until she was red, white, and blue in the face. And along comes Goody, Silverstein & Partners for the California Fluid Milk Processing Board and asks, "Got Milk?" Suddenly a white moustache is visible above the country's upper lip.

A great ad immediately resonates and gets the viewer or listener's nodding consent. It pushes a button that strikes a nerve. It evokes action in a leap that trumps logic and requires no further persuasion. That is my kind of warfare. Sure there are astronomers out there plumbing untapped solar systems, engineers devising new sources of energy, and geneticists involving themselves in the creation of life. But I'm in a different business. Mine was not to set new goals but to hammer away at preexisting ones, but put them in everyday language.

Instead of just saying municipal bonds are tax free, our headline went for the jugular and shouted, "It's crazy to throw money away." The ad does what successful advertising does. It forces the investor's nodding agreement, "Yeah, it's crazy to throw money away." And with no further persuasion, Presto! It gets the cautious, suspicious, first-time investor to grab the phone, call Lebenthal, and pour out his financial guts to a perfect stranger.

Through turbulent times, our ads have shown the newcomers to municipal bonds as awed, intimidated, unnerved, alone, vulnerable, bullish, bearish, prone to wishful thinking. And, worst of all, we have called them chrematiphobic (afraid of money). At times, we have depicted the tax-free municipal bond as a horse, a cow, and a trout. And we have portrayed interest rates as a beckoning finger, a pointy blob, and a wave traveling down a length of rope.

Depending on the environment and prevailing interest rates, we constantly adjusted our advertising. Just as a company sells a detergent by claiming it is environmentally friendly or cleaner, whiter, brighter, we skewed the message of our advertising to meet the prevailing winds. When interest rates were high, that was the time to expand the market with why you should buy municipal bonds now. So Lebenthal & Company made hay with ads in the *New York Times* featuring our "Bond of the Day," and basically let its yield speak for itself. How would newcomers to munis know where to find the Bond of the Day? We ran TV commercials promoting the *New York Times* ad on the *Today Show,* the *Early Show,* and *Good Morning America:* "You can make money before Wall Street does. If you get up, get the New York Times, and look for Lebenthal's Bond of the Day." There I was at the crack of dawn coming up out of the subway, heading for the office through the canyons of Wall Street, bending down, unlocking the front door, and brightening the ungodly hour of the morning with these immortal words "Call Lebenthal. And, if you think it's too early, you're in for a surprise. We're here now. 1-800-425-6116!"

Selling municipal bonds is easy enough when yields are a giveaway. All you have to do is run ads that are essentially saying "fresh fish" and reel them in. But when yields are down, it is a different story. Our ads then had to separate Lebenthal from the pack and fight for a larger share of a shrinking market. The message now had to be "why buy municipal bonds from Lebenthal?" What could we say about warm, human, hold-your-hand Lebenthal that no bank, no big wire house or other financial institution could say. That was when our advertising agency, Isidore Lefkowitz Elgort presented us with their creation, "At Lebenthal We Treat You Like Family!" It was how they proposed to prove it that made this one of those "Present at the Creation" moments. Celebrities would deign to call themselves Lebenthal, because we treated them so darned well we actually made them feel like one of our family.

Evolution or Intelligent Design?

Early on, I launched into Lebenthal commercials by introducing myself: "I'm Jim Lebenthal. Tax-free municipal bonds are my babies." They called me Wall Street's answer to gravel-voiced Tom Carvel and Fred the Furrier. My voice has been lambasted as nasal. (I call it reminiscent of Tony Randall's.) Critics claimed my receding hairline and angular features make me look like Frank Perdue. My tone has been described as hectoring; I prefer to think of it as hortatory. In any case, it made my radio voice as recognizable as Walter Cronkite's.

After my straight intro, I moved on to memorable high jinks. In one TV spot, accompanied by an origami cow

125

made from a municipal bond, I deadpanned, "At Lebenthal, we've been selling a cow that instead of milk gives money. A steady 9 percent a year to be precise, free of New York City, New York State, and federal income tax. So put a little moola in your portfolio and get yourself a cash cow. What would you call a bond that pays a steady tax-free income year after year? A cash cow." I also rang cowbells, tossed peanuts into my mouth, used an electrostatic generator to make my hair stand on end (lit blue from behind), and on one shot spent 67 takes throwing a bit of chalk into the air until I finally caught it on cue.

Several spots ended with a recitation of the firm's credentials. "For 60 years, through eleven recessions, three wars, the Depression, and one city crisis, we've been getting people just like you over the hurdle and finally started in tax-free municipal bonds at last."

But I get ahead of myself. We began like pretty much everyone else in our industry, running long, skinny ads in the back pages, buried in the shipping news. I called them Preparation H ads. "Did you pay needless taxes last Monday?" one asked. "How tax-free Municipal Bonds can make 1961 a tax bonus year for you," another beckoned would-be buyers. "How to keep more of your 1962 income," a third promised. Another beseeched, "Why do you ignore this income bonus?" And so on.

My first breakthrough was to go for two-column pop art cartoon ads, reducing the whole complicated business of bonds to 48 words:

Municipal Bonds. Who, Me? Municipal Bonds. Yes, Mr. Doe, you! Why share 5 percent with a tax collector, when you could be getting 7 percent tax-free and keeping it all? Get our free Municipal Bond Information Kit and start those savings earning tax-free income at the highest rate in history.

Usually, when it comes to their own money, people don't find much funny. But the pop art was zesty without being silly. And it was not silly at all when we pictured 12 digits, ten fingers and two toes, to make a point about 6 percent tax-free being the equivalent of 12 percent taxable. However, we quickly abandoned that approach. Why? Because high finance is complicated enough without demanding that your audience get the joke. We also played with and quickly dumped using Daddy Warbucks in our ads. (The "little guy" felt condescended, and the "big guy" was offended.) Yet readers' positive response to the cartoon approach—with short copy—paved the way for our going on television one day, where brevity is "burro power." And every word has to make it up and down the equivalent of the Grand Canyon with a world of meaning on its back.

The simple call to action in Lebenthal advertising has always been, "Write us, call us, or come see us for our free Municipal Bond Information Kit. It's an education in bonds that answers the questions before you ask them." Our ads grew from one column to two, then to four. I even got splashy in the *Wall Street Journal,* with a baby picture of me on my mother's lap. The headline? "Everything My Mother Taught Me about Municipal Bonds—and a Few Things She Didn't." The ad pulled 1,001 requests for Lebenthal's Municipal Bond Information Kit.

We never make cold calls at Lebenthal. Instead, we advertise the bond kit and follow up on the leads. I hate cold calls. I hate making them. I hate getting them. I hate it when strangers in the night, dialing for dollars, desecrate my dinner hour with their "bargains" in bonds. So Lebenthal became a rarity in the bond business by running provocative ads that did the reverse and made our telephone ring.

Okay. Even though I said we don't make cold calls, I did *just once* call someone out of the blue. I was trying to demonstrate the power of cheerful perseverance to a class of trainees. So I opened the phone book. I picked the first name my finger landed on and dialed. Pay dirt: A live person answered! I said, "Hello! Mister Boulduc. How are you? (affecting the bonhomie of old buddies) . . . Jim Lebenthal here of Lebenthal . . . the Municipal Bond firm."

"Oui! I know who you are," he said. "You are Jimmy Lebenthal's father. And I have your son in my French class at Trinity."

Out of the whole Manhattan phone book!

As interest rates began ratcheting up, up, up in the 1960s and 1970s, and tax-free munis beckoned to more and more savers, we went after TV watchers with a new campaign called "Lebenthal's Heroes." Each night, a different broker stood up on TV and in 30 seconds told a story about a bond that solved somebody's problem that very day:

> I was a hero today to a man who's had open heart surgery and doesn't need any extra pressure. I sold him these Hoosick Falls, New York, bonds where Grandma Moses used to paint her little cows. You never hear of

urban unrest in Hoosick Falls. But before I can recommend a "Grandma Moses Bond" for you, I have to know you, and you have to know my bonds. Call me for a free Municipal Bond Information Kit and anything the kit doesn't tell you about Municipal Bonds, I will. Because I want to be *your* hero, too.

The potent combination of a story, of real bonds for real people, of the words *Lebenthal's Heroes,* of the humanizing of municipal bonds and the mythic concept of the hero as someone who takes you by the hand and leads you from darkness to daylight, all these elements pulled together to turn municipal bonds and Lebenthal into household words.

Besides Lebenthal's Heroes, I called the stars of those commercials "My Merry Band of Players," the "Warrior Ants of the Bond Business," and finally "Financial Advisors" after "broker" became an unsavory word on Wall Street. Lebenthal brokers worked on commission. They were motivated by money—but also by something almost as compelling as the Almighty Buck: customer approval. Soon enough, our Financial Advisors grew tired of putting on makeup and hanging around for their close-ups. So I began doing most of the spots, emerging as the Lebenthal spokesperson, being recognized on the street, and getting celebrity treatment at restaurants. Ego trip? Sure, it is nice to walk into a roomful of strangers and feel universal love . . . well, almost universal. At a wedding, the great political media consultant David Garth told me he would never buy a bond from someone who advertises on TV. That's okay. I said, "I'd never vote for a candidate who advertises on TV, either."

When you've got a mundane, real boring category to sell, give it a face and personality. Call your hair dryer a "Big Boy." Dress up those rubber tires as "Road Grippers." Go out with a camera and shoot a team of mighty workhorses plowing the farm at sunrise, and record a guy with a basso profundo voice declaring, "At Lebenthal, we see tax-free municipal bonds as the workhorse of investments. Because after 200 years, eight wars, four depressions, 20 recessions, and one city crisis, the municipal bond is still building our cities and towns and paying the kind of tax-free income no bank can give you. At Lebenthal, we still believe in America's workhorse."

A Dog-Eat-Dog-Food World

One evening, with the Great Inflation raging outside, I found myself idling in the office with Jeff Harrison, the last broker to leave for home. I dropped into a chair. "How'd you do today? Sell anything?" Jeff shook his head and put on the crestfallen look of self-rebuke a sales-free day brings. We had been advertising municipal bond yields on radio and TV of 12 percent and more—triple tax-free! Really! You would think 12 percent bonds would fly right out the window. But with the Consumer Price Index then at 15 percent, even 12 percent would be a game for losers if inflation stayed in the double digits.

Because advertising legends are peopled with ordinary folks coming up with killer copy (e.g., "Ham What Am!" from Louise Beavers mouth to Cary Grant's ear in *Mr. Blandings Builds His Dream House*), I asked this broker,

Jeff, to tell me what I could say in an ad to make his clients focus on the cash flow from the 12 percent coupon and not just on the cash-in value of the bond at maturity when who knew what the dollar would be worth?

Jeff's answer? "Beats me!" Which is okay. Someone to talk to is part of the creative process. And besides, I'm inspired by faces just begging to be lit up. Jeff, my silent collaborator, triggered the memory of an article I had seen in the *Wall Street Journal* talking about a "cash cow." And thus, Lebenthal's Cash Cow came into being.

I don't care who the father of the idea is. Jeff gets the credit. Half of winning is just showing up. And Jeff showed up that day.

Here is another ad that made the phone ring during a slump when the bond market was so quiet the traders could hear the blood rushing through their own temples: "Once Alberta Gim didn't know anybody in the bond business, but she knew it was crazy to keep throwing money away. So she got to know somebody. Us! And you should, too."

It came from two different thoughts from two different agencies. The first thought, "It's crazy to throw money away," was the brainchild of Grace and Rothschild.

Roy Grace and Diane Rothschild were two advertising greats from the grand old days of Doyle Dane Bernbach. They had formed their own agency all the while swearing to themselves never to take crap from another client. I was their second account, Land Rover their first. Land Rover got award-winning advertising featuring a mud-splattered Range Rover. I got a commercial showing people literally throwing money away. It was so vulgar, especially the fat man flushing money down the toilet, that in the screening room Sayra Lebenthal dropped her head low and said, "I'd hang my head in shame if that ever ran on TV."

The second thought came from a casual remark made by an agency pitching our account. They said, "At one time in their lives, none of your customers knew the name Lebenthal." Bingo! A light went on. And I put the two thoughts together in a gangbuster commercial showing Alberta Gim and a bunch of other Lebenthal customers who got to know us because they knew it was crazy to throw money away.

I superimposed on the screen the actual bonds the clients had just bought—name, coupon, and maturity. Forgive the disrespect, but in ad-speak it's called "Showing the dogs eating the dog food."

Client Non Grata

There are executives who have reputations as fearsome as the Grim Reaper: Sydney Greenstreet in *The Hucksters,* playing the fictional counterpart of American Tobacco tycoon George Washington Hill; Edgar Bronfman Sr. of Seagram's; "Chainsaw Al" Dunlop of Sunbeam; Linda "Hell-on-Heels" Wachner of the Warnaco Group. In the fancy suites along Madison Avenue, I was known as the Client from Hades. After I had more accounts with advertising agencies than Larry King had wives, it got so when I called new agencies about handling Lebenthal, their new business directors began telling their secretaries, "Tell him I called in dead."

The best way I know to wreck the relationship between client and agency is to love advertising too much and become convinced that the great American municipal bond ad is there in the agency somewhere, floating around like Tinkerbell. These guys better find it. Because I will not run an ad that I don't think is great.

In spite of my hand on the scalpel and my finger meddling in the pie. Lebenthal has been blessed with great advertising, beginning with Albert Frank-Guenther Law (AFGL) in the 1960s. The elevator groaned and the floorboards creaked at this fuddy-duddy shop that produced tombstone ads for financial deals and offerings. But I would walk in on a Thursday with an idea. And a day later, I would be up at the *New York Times* with a knockoff of Roy Lichtenstein's pop art, eyes burning to know, "Why isn't there a municipal bond in every home in America?" for the Sunday business section. My two-column-by-seven-inch cartoon ad absolutely dominated that full newspaper page. Cause of divorce? I ran out of ideas. And the AFGL team had virtually none of its own.

What pop art was able to do in one-ninth of a page took my next agency, fresh, insolent Calderhead Jackson, a full page in the early 1970s. But their gutsy plain talk ("Basic Arithmetic Tells You When You Don't Belong in a Bank") and lengthy copy letting the reader know where babies come from, made municipal bonds spectacular and Lebenthal exciting. Dick Jackson and Dick Calderhead who ran the agency, now kaput, wrote, "New York's Streets Should Be as Safe as Its Bonds." Cause of divorce: politics. My partner couldn't stand their imperiousness. I couldn't stand my partner's complaining about them. It is always the agency that goes, never the partner.

I still love the work that another agency, Case & Mc-Grath, turned out, positioning us as leaders with big balls. "Once again, Lebenthal shocks the bond establishment." "Lebenthal uncovers the secret column of Municipal Bond prices." Make news, then run ads about it. I blew our relationship by changing the copy and assignment so often that its chief executive, Pat McGrath, fired *me* to restore morale in the agency and to keep creative director Gene Case from crawling up the wall.

Twice I switched to Isidore Lefkowitz Elgort. The first time around, the firm presented Lebenthal's salespeople as heroes—but then the city plunged into a fiscal crisis, and the heroes became goats. Although my bonds paid in full and on time, market values fell more than 30 percent and I could hear my clients' interior monologue begging me to make them whole. Listening to their thinking, I quietly killed the campaign. But the agency scored again with their "Why buy municipal bonds from Lebenthal?" campaign that turned celebrities into family members. Count Basie called himself Count Lebenthal, Joan Fontaine became Joan Lebenthal, June Lockhart was suddenly June Lebenthal, all to make the point that at Lebenthal we treat our customers like family. There was only one problem: The agency couldn't take "yes" for an answer. Somehow they couldn't bring their own concept to life. I took over the writing, production, and execution of their idea. For a while, we paid the agency its commission on ads that ran, until enough was enough, and we pocketed the 15 percent.

Like the Shah of Iran having to dump his Queen Soraya for not producing a male heir, I dumped Chiat-Day after intense love-making with no son to show for it. I never got a taste of the great advertising they turned out for Apple to introduce the MAC: "Why 1984 won't be like *1984*." Or the fantastic municipal bond ads they turned out for Drexel Burnham a few months after we split. Perhaps if I had waited . . . but I had no time. I needed to make a difference in financial advertising . . . now!

I was notorious for being my own worst client—I was even voted "Worst Client of the Year" by a major ad magazine, topping even Mars, which made its agency people sample the cat food, and Gallo, which made their hapless creative teams stand in the sweltering Modesto parking lot for hours before granting them an audience. But I was a unique client who finally got stuck with himself, and for 25 years, has been president, copy chief, and sole client of Lebenthal, The Ad Agency, Inc., the in-house advertising agency that I created out of desperation.

Someone Who Lasted Longer Than a Day

Then, Alakazam! Out of an orange-colored sky came a former Good Humor Man, Ron Holland—the Gilbert to my Sullivan, the Damon to my Pythias, the Royal Mountie to my Albert Lasker. Back in 1904, Albert Lasker was the head of a very tame, very successful advertising agency, Lord & Thomas (even though Lasker really didn't know what advertising was). He found out one historic day, when a business card landed on his desk from a former Royal Canadian Mountie waiting in the bar downstairs. It said, "I know what advertising is. If you want to find out, send my card back down. Signed, John Kennedy."

At a time when advertising consisted of naming the product, telling its price, and explaining its purpose, Kennedy had exactly three magic words to describe advertising: "Salesmanship in Print." Those three words became Lasker's mantra. And he and his agency, Lord & Thomas, became the founders of modern advertising. When radio changed the world, they expanded "Salesmanship in Print" to include the new medium and invented the commercial and the sponsored radio show. Families soon huddled around the radio to hear *Amos 'n Andy,* brought to listeners six nights a week by Pepsodent. American streets emptied, traffic disappeared, even movie attendance was disrupted. Everything stopped except Pepsodent sales. Advertising created to sell changed the United States and reshaped the whole country's culture.

Ron Holland was my Royal Canadian Mountie and Albert Lasker rolled into one. Before cajoling children with his Good-Humor shout of "Chocolate Chip, Chocolate Malt, Toasted Almond, Coconut, Strawberry, Banana, Red Raspberry, and the Weekly Special," he had been a counterintelligence agent, a copywriter, the founder and copy chief of his own hot advertising agency in the 1980s, Lois

Holland Callaway. He was the man behind the image of Joe Baum's restaurants, The Four Seasons, Charlie O's, The Rainbow Room, Windows on the World . . . and, for America's Bicentennial, inventor of the $19.76 lunch available at the swankiest eateries in the city (increased by one penny a year). So this year, those famous bargain lunches are selling for only $20.06. Better hurry! 2007 is right around the corner.

A master of letters, lyrics, and salesmanship in print, radio, and TV, Ron has collaborated with me on every Lebenthal ad, newsletter, and even personal letters for the past 15 years. How does the sharpest wit, quickest mind, and fastest draw in advertising shoot it out with his favorite worst client of the year? In the next chapter, come along and sit in on dinner at City Hall Restaurant in lower Manhattan and hear us thrash out the creation of Lebenthal's latest TV campaign: "Maybe We're Just a Little Bit Better." Even though the chapter seems to be about Ron and me, agent and client, talking ad copy, it is really about the little things that count and made us what we are today.

LEBENTHAL TO GO

A brand is earned.
It's the public's gift to
you for being good.

Advertising is the hammer
that nails your message home.
A great ad often hands
the hammer to the consumer
to complete the thought.

Don't be afraid to take leaps
of logic or imagination.
If your ad pushes the button,
consumers will make the leap
right along with you.

CEOs seldom understand advertising.
It's the first thing they go for
when cutting expenses.
Advertising isn't an expense.
It's an investment in your brand.

It makes no difference if you
have a lowly job like mangling sheets
in the steam laundry,
pretend you are an advertising genius
and turn mangling sheets into
the greatest thing since sliced bread.

9

Creating the "Little Bit Better" Campaign

Two grown men, a 77-year-old jut-jawed businessman, in a long face and double-breasted pin stripe, and the other, a wisecracking 74-year-old writer in a sport jacket and sneakers, sit cattycorner to each other, having drinks, dinner, and laughs at City Hall Restaurant, 139 Duane Street in Lower Manhattan. Outside, the pall of 9/11 may still hang over Lower Manhattan. But inside City Hall the mood at our table is definitely "boys will be boys." Something is afoot. A video cameraman is parked at the table documenting our every word. That is because Ron Holland and I are going to create Lebenthal & Company's next great advertising campaign (the same way I remember the Firestone Tire and Rubber Company making a tire before your eyes at the 1939 World Fair). Although Ron and I know we are on camera, we quickly become ourselves and dive into the business of making jokes and cracking the other up. In other words, "creation." Never you mind. There never was a more serious business dinner. And I have every intention of putting the receipt into Lebenthal & Company for legitimate reimbursement. Read, and you will see why.

HOLLAND: What are we doing?

LEBENTHAL: Writing a commercial: you saying one thing and me saying no, that's not it, and you saying another. And in the process, capturing some of the humor, some of the bonhomie that you and I have been generating for 15 years—of trying to get people over their hangup: "Not now, I'll wait. Interest rates are going up."

HOLLAND: That's always been your problem.

LEBENTHAL: The words haven't been written that can make someone buy one minute before they're good and ready. Maybe we're gonna end up deciding the only thing that we can do in advertising is offer people an education in the bonds. Anything other than that— teaching them how to buy the most un-understood investment in America—is just barking up a tree.

HOLLAND: What do you mean—?

LEBENTHAL: People think they don't understand the bonds. One reason they think they don't understand them is that they bring the values of the stock market to bonds, and they complicate their lives. They think they're supposed to buy low, sell high, and make money timing the market. For 2 percent plain, they can't bring themselves to understand. Maybe the challenge for Lebenthal is to upgrade the people skills of the broker you get on the telephone when you call. That person has to be some-one who can define you to a *T* no matter what your problem is and what the problems of the market at the moment are and tell you what your strategy ought to be. Bonds aren't always going to be the answer. No to bonds could mean yes to equities . . . insurance . . . annuities.

HOLLAND: What we say all the time is "that's what we do best . . . help people decide yes or no," right?

LEBENTHAL: Yes . . .

HOLLAND: So—

LEBENTHAL: A no should be a segue into a yes to something else . . . a strategy, a plan. It would be a shame if we couldn't find your need and fill it.

HOLLAND: Nothing's going to pay more than the bond.

LEBENTHAL: If I were sure that I had someone on the tele-phone who just had to squeeze the bull off the nickel, then I'd know how to function. There are hedges and strategies for the "yield hog." But, yield is not everything.

HOLLAND: Why would I ever say, "Gee I don't want that much yield, give me less?"

LEBENTHAL: Because of the risk.

HOLLAND: Okay. All right. So it's always a trade-off.

LEBENTHAL: There's risk and there's risk. Default is rarely the problem. The problem is loss of market value—market risk. That's what can kill you.

HOLLAND: We were talking about how to get people off the dime, right?

LEBENTHAL: Yes.

HOLLAND: They're sitting around saying well, you know, I just sense interest rates are going to go up. Even Alan Greenspan's stumped. You can't watch television or read a newspaper without being told interest rates are going up. They haven't gone up and they should have. Greenspan called it a "conundrum."

LEBENTHAL: One reason they haven't gone up is demand: from baby boomers investing for their retirement, for cash flow in retirement. Like everybody else, they are disgusted with equities. They've lost their shirts in the stock market. And they are buying bonds.

HOLLAND: So it's a marvelous moment for bonds.

LEBENTHAL: Longer than a moment, Ron. I say that it's going to be several years of marvelous moments. Now I don't say that in public because I have no way of knowing.

HOLLAND: Well, of course you do. You're an authority.

LEBENTHAL: Yeah, my belief is my authority. Assertion is my proof. Only God can say where interest rates are going. . . . God . . . Volcker . . . or a wonderful home-spun philosopher like Will Rogers. . . . An actor like Hal Holbrook doing Will Rogers. What a spokesperson for Lebenthal that would be!

FEMALE VOICE: Welcome to City Hall.

HOLLAND: Oh, I didn't realize this restaurant had such magnificent-looking staff.

FEMALE VOICE: May I start you gentlemen this evening with sparkling or flat water?

HOLLAND: Oh, I'm not going to have any water. Save that for under a bridge or something. But I will have a glass of red wine. What can I have, except for Merlot?

FEMALE VOICE: Okay. We have a great [unintelligible], Silverado cabernet zinfandel and a fantastic [unintelligible] burgundy.

HOLLAND: Burgundy.

FEMALE VOICE: Something for you, sir?

LEBENTHAL: I'm going to have a white wine.

FEMALE VOICE: Okay.

LEBENTHAL: And say my choices.

FEMALE VOICE: [Unintelligible] a chardonnay. We also have a [unintelligible] it's a little sweeter than a riesling.

LEBENTHAL: Okay. I am going to have the second one you mentioned.

FEMALE VOICE: The chardonnay?

LEBENTHAL: No, I forgot what it was.

FEMALE VOICE: Sauvignon blanc?

LEBENTHAL: Was that the second? Yeah. Yeah. Pinot grigio, sauvignon blanc. I'm going to have a sauvignon blanc.

FEMALE VOICE: Okay.

HOLLAND: Would Ben (Ben Hayflick, the cameraman) like a drink?

LEBENTHAL: He can't have a drink, he's shooting. . . . Ron, you have to give people calling in a strategy that permits them to save and invest in all markets. We came up with a message for Alexandra that says it's always the right time for munis, because they're always priced to beat the alternative in high tax brackets.

HOLLAND: Right. So what is our dilemma?

LEBENTHAL: Our dilemma is that when rates are 2 percent, it makes no difference that 2 percent beats 1 percent. The 100 percent by which 2 percent beats 1 percent is of no real appeal. Who cares about the relative yield when the actual return stinks. There's no incentive even to lick the stamp and send for the bond kit.

HOLLAND: But that can't be so because people are buying bonds every day from you, right? So they're not saying it stinks.

LEBENTHAL: Thank you, you're absolutely right. So I ask myself, what is it that makes the guy who's got money now, invest now at whatever the rate? Years ago we did a campaign when nobody was buying. God, it was quiet and lonely in the office. I could hear the blood rushing through my temples. Nobody was buying, that is, except for someone here and someone there, one or two people.

HOLLAND: Right.

LEBENTHAL: What did they know nobody else knew? And that's where the commercial, "Once Alberta Gim didn't know anybody in the bond business" came from. "But she knew it was crazy to keep throwing money away, so she got to know somebody, us." We made getting to know Lebenthal a proxy for getting off your ass. And we actually superimposed a description of the bond she just bought on the screen.

HOLLAND: And that didn't turn anyone?

LEBENTHAL: It was a great, great market turner-arounder.

HOLLAND: Run it again.

LEBENTHAL: You mean repeat an old successful Lebenthal campaign? That would be cheating, a violation of the honor code.

HOLLAND: No it's not. No, no, no. It's saying that sitting there and doing nothing is throwing money away. And that's crazy when I can beat whatever you're getting now. You're above repeating your most basic, persuasive advertising message?

LEBENTHAL: I've got to think about that. What I really want to do is talk to present bond investors. I'd like to get present buyers away from Morgan Stanley and Smith Barney, because you know present buyers have the money.

HOLLAND: Well, why would anyone leave Morgan Stanley and come to Lebenthal . . . that's what you want to say then, right? We're running a little late, folks, so good-night . . . [Laughter]. Well, if I have my money with Morgan Stanley, and I'm already in munis there's nothing in that bond kit I have to know, is there?

LEBENTHAL: Basically you're right. You may not know a damn thing, but you don't feel the need to know. Your ignorance is bliss. The kit promises an education, which is fine when interest rates go up and it's time to expand the market. The higher yields reach out to newcomers in lower tax brackets for whom tax-frees held no benefit before. But now in this low interest rate environment, it's time to get you away from Morgan Stanley and for us to increase market share. Why leave your present broker and come to Lebenthal? It's the most fun, creative, and difficult advertising there is. But do it right and its stealing fire from the gods.

HOLLAND: What right do I have asking you to leave your present broker or your present bond company? Only one. Only one. Maybe we're just a little bit better. It'd be great if you had some evidence of that. How much did you win your Olympic swimming medal by? By the $\frac{1}{10}$th, $\frac{1}{100}$th, $\frac{1}{10,000}$th of a second. You were just that much better.

LEBENTHAL: That's marvelous. Avis made a company out of America's love of the underdog: "We're only number two."

HOLLAND: No, they said we try harder, big difference, enormous difference. It was marvelous advertising. You really thought, "Oh, I bet they do clean the mirror. Oh, I bet they do, you know, fill it up with gas."

LEBENTHAL: All you have to do is clean the goddamn mirror.

HOLLAND: Yeah. And empty the ashtray. Now, if you really want credibility, suppose you say "maybe." Maybe we're just a little bit better. Not a ton, a little bit. You're not trying to win the Kentucky Derby.

LEBENTHAL: Yeah.

HOLLAND: Sam Goldwyn advanced $25,000 to the playwrights Ben Hecht and Charles MacArthur to bring him a screenplay. When the money was spent and their time was up, Goldwyn asked, "What have you two geniuses created?" MacArthur told him they were finishing a script on Vaslav Nijinsky. "Nijinksy? Who's this Nijinsky?" Sam asked. "Oh," MacArthur explained, "Nijinsky was the greatest dancer that ever lived. All of Europe was at his feet . . . but at the height of his fame, he went crazy and spent the rest of his life in an insane asylum convinced that he was a horse!"

Goldwyn blew his stack. "I give you $25 thousand and you come back with a furshuginer story about some faggot dancer who thinks he's a horse? Get out of here!" And Goldwyn starts throwing stuff at them. They're ducking and trying to get out of the door. MacArthur turned back to Goldwyn and said, "Sam! If you want a happy ending . . . we could have him win the Kentucky Derby." [Laughter]

LEBENTHAL: I knew Goldwyn. I actually heard him say a Sam Goldwynism: The movie of *Guys and Dolls* was not going to be a cardboard copy of the original. Carbon copy? . . . carbon? cardboard? . . .

HOLLAND: But you have to give an example of being a little better. You could say, "You know what? I'm just as happy at the end of the day when a customer says no as when they say yes if they say it because they've listened to me." You can do a thing how the words in the bond kit make sure people understand . . . how we bond with you, the family thing, how we help you decide yes . . . or no.

LEBENTHAL: A campaign built on how we're just a little bit better than all those guys with the zeroes and commas after their name. I love it.

HOLLAND: It's the little—

LEBENTHAL: I liked it when you said the $\frac{1}{10,000}$th.

HOLLAND: Do you realize in a dead calm if the Queen Elizabeth was in the middle of the Hudson River, you could pull that ship into shore with a number 10 thread. You could because there's a little bit more influence on this side than there is on the other side. [Unintelligible] Of course, in a hurricane, not so good.

LEBENTHAL: All things being equal, that little bit better is the butterfly flapping its wings in Beijing that creates a storm in New York.

HOLLAND: You know it as soon as you talk to your first Lebenthal broker. You know how grandmas will say, "It's the little things that count."

LEBENTHAL: Being a little bit better and demonstrating it. . . . It's all up to whom you get on the phone when you call Lebenthal.

147

HOLLAND: Right.

LEBENTHAL: This is fantastic. I know because the waitress always manages to come just as soon as we're onto something.

FEMALE VOICE: We do have a few specials this evening. We have a chilled gazpacho soup with cucumbers, tomatoes, and garnished with corn tortillas. Our special salad this evening is jumbo [unintelligible] served with avocado and tart plums, and our special fish is a salt-crusted [unintelligible] that is oven baked and served with a side of Dijon hollandaise sauce.

LEBENTHAL: Let me have the first two.

FEMALE VOICE: All right.

LEBENTHAL: The gazpacho and the what?

FEMALE VOICE: The shrimp.

LEBENTHAL: Then I don't know what I'm gonna have after that.

HOLLAND: Well, that's enough for the moment isn't it? Two courses? None of my business.

LEBENTHAL: One is a soup and one's a salad.

FEMALE VOICE: You can always get some sides for the table.

LEBENTHAL: Yeah. Okay. Exactly. Exactly. And your sides are what?

FEMALE VOICE: Mashed potatoes, curried onion rings, hash browns, french fries, cream spinach. Two special ones that have just been added to the menu are sugar snap peas that are cooked in butter and shallots.

LEBENTHAL: Sold American. . . . And I'm going to have another of these very fine, oh—[Inaudible]

FEMALE VOICE: Sauvignon blanc.

LEBENTHAL: Good.

HOLLAND: I'll have another one of these, too.

FEMALE VOICE: Okay. Great.

HOLLAND: It'd be interesting if we could think of some real, happy Lebenthal family customers who'd say I think they're just a little bit better.

LEBENTHAL: Stay with Alexandra as the spokesperson.

HOLLAND: Right.

LEBENTHAL: Nobody believes endorsements, nobody, unless you get, you know, Martha Stewart to endorse ankle bracelets or something, then they get attention.

HOLLAND: That's not true. What you just said isn't true. I'll tell you endorsement. When Kennedy was running against Nixon, they both came off a plane. They met in the airport, two different planes and they both had Richard Neustadt's book, *Presidential Power,* they both had it on them. That boosted those sales a lot. But now you've done it. You've killed it. No endorsements.

LEBENTHAL: Well, let me try to think of ways that we are better, and—

HOLLAND: Well, one very important way is saying, is telling them it's okay to decide no. No one else does that.

LEBENTHAL: Giving investors the information they need to make an informed decision—yes or no—is what full disclosure and fair dealing are all about.

HOLLAND: I know, I know. You're taking ownership of what the rules require you to do by inviting the customer to turn you thumbs down. But as soon as Lebenthal starts saying they do that, it separates you. Are we miles ahead of everybody else? Are we mountaintops better? Are we five tons better? No. We're just a little bit better. And in the long run, it is the little things that count.

149

LEBENTHAL: I think it's so great, because I'll tell you, in the old days it was delivering your bonds to you on Christmas Eve so you could hand them out the next day to the grandchildren.

HOLLAND: I like that.

LEBENTHAL: Well there are no physical bond certificates to hand out anymore, but it was things like that. It was the letters that I do get from people who are so grateful that we called them even to sell them a bond. They're grateful that we do our job.

HOLLAND: They're grateful you knew they were alive.

LEBENTHAL: This gazpacho could be a little bit—could be a little bit better.

HOLLAND: Could be a little colder do you think?

LEBENTHAL: No.

HOLLAND: Well, these plums are very tart, she was right about that.

LEBENTHAL: Now let me ask you something, what do we do at this point? Quit and say, we got it?

HOLLAND: No.

LEBENTHAL: Huh?

HOLLAND: No. You decide what the examples are going to be. Examples that maybe are just a little bit better than I got from my old place.

LEBENTHAL: Do we have to say the "maybe?"

HOLLAND: Why do people come to you for their heart transplant? Because maybe I'm just a little bit better. They don't say 'cause I'm better. There!

LEBENTHAL: But without the maybe. . . . When I say we're just a little bit better without equivocating. . . .

HOLLAND: Swell, say it without the maybe and turn a credible, unpretentious statement of fact into an extravagant advertising claim.

LEBENTHAL: Ron, say it both ways. Maybe we're just a little bit better. Now say, we're just a little bit better. . . .

HOLLAND: No you say it. Maybe we're just a little bit better said with self-assurance and good nature means you're a lot better. Because it is the little things that count. Joe Baum did an ad for the Newarka Restaurant that said, "The Newarka is probably the nicest restaurant in New Jersey." Joe said: Could you take probably out? [Laughter] Joe, just think of it, "The Newarka is the nicest restaurant in New Jersey. Well, isn't that interesting?" [Crosstalk]

LEBENTHAL: Could we rob Joe's grave and say we're probably a little bit better? "Probably" is more considered and becoming of a distinguished bond firm. "Maybe" is more, "Aw Gee, I dunno."

HOLLAND: Sure you could say "probably," as long as you say it disarmingly. Probably we're a little bit better. All you want to do is get the license to say a little bit better. But if you say we're a little bit better, that's just puffery. But if you say, "Why do they come to us? Because maybe we're just a little bit better, or we're probably a little bit better, could it possibly be that we're a little bit better?" As long as you say it with that disarming tone, it means you are. You have to fight enormous companies and extraordinary competition with a unique human touch.

LEBENTHAL: I was just going to tell you about spilling coffee on my client's shirt. I sent my sales assistant to the back to get some soap and water and personally removed the spot. In the two minutes it took, he lost $2 million, because my eye wasn't on the ticker. But his shirt looked like new. Is it possible, could it be, just perhaps, that we're just a little bit better every which what way?

HOLLAND: No. No. No. Not in every way. Only in the extra minutes we put into everything because our computers are so slow. [Laughter]

LEBENTHAL: How did you make that leap from Good Humor Man to whatever, to advertising?

HOLLAND: My brother Jack said you're too old to be a Good Humor Man. You don't look cute anymore. He said, you can either become an actor or go into advertising, and there's an outfit, I don't know the name of them, but they did the advertising for Dilly Beans, string beans pickled in dill. The radio commercial said if your friendly neighborhood grocer doesn't have Dilly Beans when you ask for them; knock something off the shelf on the way out. [Laughter] Jack said find out who that is and send in a resume. Papert, Koenig & Lois. I sent them a short story. Their secretary said you know, we usually throw things like that right out, but I didn't, I don't know why. Anyway, Julian Koenig agreed to see me, and the rest was hysteria.

LEBENTHAL: In case you say anything useful, can I bring your mike up higher? In your opinion what is the first decent thing you wrote that made the airwaves?

HOLLAND: I did a Preparation H spot. I did, and they wouldn't run it.

LEBENTHAL: What? If you don't like it, shove it up your ass?

HOLLAND: No, it wasn't vulgar. It was kiss swollen hemorrhoids goodbye.

LEBENTHAL: Are you pulling my leg? Ron, I'm sitting here thinking of what we achieved tonight about little things counting?

HOLLAND: We're still here after 80 years because it's the little things that count. How come the big guys haven't taken over all the business? You all sell the same commodity. Money! You all use the same nine digits and a zero. In a service business, it's the ashtrays, the mirror—the service that counts. Maybe, just maybe, it's how you treat clients that makes you a little bit better.

LEBENTHAL: I will execute what you say brilliantly. By the way, I don't see you taking a single note. Those pencils have not been dulled by a single dipthong.

HOLLAND: Diphthong, diphthong. It's not dipthong. It's diphtheria. Did you stifle a yawn? I think you did.

LEBENTHAL: No, I did not stifle a yawn.

HOLLAND: You should never do that.

LEBENTHAL: Alexandra's the person to do the commercial.

HOLLAND: It would be perfect for her because it would ameliorate some of the necessity to be all business and capture the twinkle.

LEBENTHAL: If we did it as a TV spot—

HOLLAND: Yes, oh you do, 'cause that's how you telegraph the twinkle. And the mildest sort of claim becomes extraordinary.

LEBENTHAL: Why is a claim of a miniscule superiority—

HOLLAND: Because it is absolute superiority. All you have to do is be better. We're not talking a very complicated stretch of logic: If the count had been 12 seconds, I wouldn't have been knocked out. But it is 10 seconds, and we didn't see you get up. The first commercial we did at Lois Holland Calloway was with Joe Louis. To our generation, Joe Louis was the champion of all—better than Babe Ruth, better than Mickey Mantle, better than Ted Williams, better than Jesse Owens.

Jim Calloway, George Lois, and I hired him to do a commercial for a small stock brokerage house called Edwards and Hanley. And all Joe had to do was sit there, and just say "Edwards and Hanley, where were you when I needed you?"

Everyone knew Joe was a champion for 11 years; he made $4 million and he'd been screwed out of all of it, including by the government. He fought for four years during the war, he turned over all his purses, all his purses to the United Army Fund, and the government said oh that's still income though. You've got to pay taxes on that. It was just unbelievable.

Anyway, when we had him there and cued him, he was supposed to say, "Edwards and Hanley, where were you when I needed you?" But Joe said, "Where was you when I needed you?" In those days, we couldn't let him be ungrammatical. We're going to get killed for that. I said, "Joe, they had trouble with the sound, they didn't hear a word." So we cut it in half and all he had to say was, "Where were you when I needed you?" Okay. Could we do it again? He said, "Okay. Where was you when I needed you?" I said to the sound guy, "How's that? Did we get all that? Oh, we still haven't got it? Don't ask me why, Joe. They're having trouble in the booth with 'were,' so you've really got to hit that." Joe said, "Okay, how I say it?" I said, "You got to say Edwards and Hanley, where were you when I needed you? Okay?" So then he said, "Okay, roll it. Edwards and Hanley, where was you at?" [Laughter] So we finally just clipped the S off the was, so he said, "Where wa you when I needed you?" But I mean he knew. . . . It was so was perfect.

FEMALE VOICE: Just to let you know, our fruit du jour is fresh watermelon, pink and yellow, and that is served with strawberries.

HOLLAND: What kind of dog do you think they have to guard the fields where these melons are grown?

LEBENTHAL: What kind of dog?

HOLLAND: Melon collies. Melancholies.

LEBENTHAL: Ron, I want to get a spot on the air . . . just so we get a spot out of this evening. . . .

HOLLAND: Speaking of spot, somebody saw Helen Keller crossing the street with her dog. And the dog lifted his leg and pissed on her leg. She reached in her pocketbook and gave it a treat. And this guy said, "Lady I don't know if you realize that dog just pissed on your leg?" She said, "I know, I gotta find out where its mouth is so I can kick him in the ass." [Laughter] True story!

LEBENTHAL: Ron, what is the process by which now we're going to get a spot that is on the air, that—

HOLLAND: It's back and forth. It's back and forth. It's butting heads with you, saying to each other over and over again, "What are we really trying to say? . . . How can we make Lebenthal seem different?" I'll try to insist on the maybe thing. And you'll say fine but we've got to have this, we've got to have that. . . . Don't forget, most of the stuff that appears on the air, you did.

155

LEBENTHAL: Oh, that's not right, you can't say that. You can't say that.

HOLLAND: I believe I just did. Didn't I, Ben?

BEN: I have it on tape.

LEBENTHAL: Your contribution to the collaborative process—is that of the La Brea Tar Pits to the saber-toothed tiger. The—

FEMALE VOICE: . . . complimentary cookies . . . chocolate chip, chocolate chocolate chip, coconut macaroon, pecan sandies, and peanut butter.

HOLLAND: Great timing. All you ever need to get the attention of your waiter is be in the middle of a story. It's the thing with George Lois and I. You and I do the same thing, which is never be embarrassed to bring up an idea. It is very, very important.

LEBENTHAL: Yeah.

HOLLAND: It really is. You see, it doesn't matter how awful, how rotten, how corny, how stiff, how overworked, how retarded, just being able to throw anything out, and when you do, that's when you move to the right side of the brain when everything happens in a flash of lightning really.

LEBENTHAL: Exactly my analogy to the La Brea Tar Pits burbling and coughing up the fang of a saber-toothed tiger that you can use. An old bicycle wheel. A bon mot. A piece of usage. But then it's your words that push the button that with no further persuasion evokes a leap of logic: "It's the little things that count."

HOLLAND: Right. Tell the truth, make it interesting. That's all advertising is. Ever!

LEBENTHAL: Ron, I think we've beaten the horse. . . .

HOLLAND: If you think about it, that is why Lebenthal not only endures but prevails, because, you know, we really are a little bit better . . . because my mother and father were in it . . . because I came back, and turned the company over to my daughter. It's because some of our people, who may not be MBAs, still answer your questions, make sure you understand, and are not just out to make a sale, but really help you decide "yes . . . or no" and make it a pleasure to do business with Lebenthal . . . if nothing else, because they have that Lebenthal touch and just maybe are a little bit better.

LEBENTHAL: That's a wrap. Room tone! The tar pit has gurgled.

LEBENTHAL TO GO

Don't be afraid of throwing an idea on the table. One of those mud-covered oysters might have a pearl in it.

When you're afraid a headline is too daring, make believe your competitor ran it.

How are you doing on that ad about the steam laundry? Have you decided whether to sell the idea of sending linens out to be laundered? Or sending them out to be laundered at your particular laundry?

10

Who Is That Guy up There?

Stepping up to the podium with my speech in pocket for the kickoff breakfast of the 1994 U.S. Conference of Mayors in Portland, Oregon (right after President Clinton had just greeted them over the PA system), I asked myself, "Who the hell am I to be telling these guys how to run their business?" I'm a bond salesman. So I've spent over a million a year in self-promotion. Suppose I woke up one morning and discovered nobody knew me? And the hand of God came down out of the sky, pointed right at me and said, "You're never going to be on TV again, Jim Lebenthal?"

It would be a little like visiting my wife Jackie's folks in Twin Falls, Idaho, where I am known only as the husband from back East in New York of Dr. Beymer's little girl, Jackie. Obscurity like that always triggers the wisenheimer in me. When the head of the Idaho State Guard asked me how would I like to live in a small town like Twin Falls,

I answered, "I wouldn't like to live in one, Sir, but I'd sure like to own one." Da-dum!

I know why I am a sought after breakfast speaker: I know how to wake up an audience. But I would have to say that I am more of an acquired taste than someone out of one of those speakers bureau catalogues would be, like, say, Bill Cosby.

At the Mayor's Conference, my way around a Bill Cosby's unavailability was to slip whoever was introducing me a short short introduction that would make the mayors feel they hadn't been watching the right TV shows and that they were the ones out of the know:

And now the man who made the municipal bonds of your hometowns famous, someone whose name is a household word wherever his voice is heard and whose face is seen on radio and TV: Jim (Built by Bonds) Lebenthal.

After that, I walked up to the microphone, and gave those mayors a stump speech that trumped the best of the stumpers among them:

Greetings, my fellow municipal bond "wonks."
That's better than a lot of the things they call you.
Yes? Why would anyone want to be a mayor,
when our cities are so ungovernable? Do you get
that a lot in Anaheim, Azusa, and Cucamonga, or
only in New York City, where I come from? You
know where Jack Benny got those names from?
Clipping his coupons in the vault one day—from

his Anaheim, Azusa, and Cucamonga municipal bonds.

You could feel the audience waking up and getting curious: "Who is that guy up there?" The very question I asked myself, rolling over in bed the other night, trying to find the sweet spot where my arm wasn't in the way, so I could recall the plateaus of my awareness in growing up, like tying my own shoelaces, diving feet first off the high board, taking off from a cow pasture for a $2 ride with a barnstormer. How much of who you are do you take with you to the podium?

Mr. Mayor, Madam Mayor, you could use help, couldn't you? I mean it's ugly out there: potholes, poverty, crime, drugs, snow removal, AIDS, homelessness, pollution, urban decay, hazardous wastes, jails, jobs, education, health care, welfare—oh, occasionally getting a cat down from a tree—the whole domestic agenda. Those are your problems to solve at the state and local level. In the 1930s, in the Depression, we turned to Washington—not the states—to rebuild America. I don't have to tell you that today Uncle Sam is broke and downloading his responsibilities onto your shoulders.

I am an expert on downloading. I once downloaded the savings from my sister Eleanor's coin bank. It was a silvery metal tube with a slit near the top for inserting dimes that could be accessed with a jimmy. So this Jimmy helped himself to 10 cents here, 10 cents there as the need arose for inconspicuous consumption. I was undone by a roll of Life

Savers on my person that I couldn't possibly have bought with earnings from my paper route, not having a paper route or any other means of support at the age of five.

The mayors also had a powerful tool for downloading the nation's savings and using our unspent incomes to re-build America and get this magnificent country of ours off its magnificent bottom—their power to borrow in the low-cost tax-free bond market. I love debt. And I told them so:

Debt! Good debt that adds to the sum of our great public works. Not bad debt that just adds to deficits. I love debt for projects that yield a positive payback for many years to come. Let me give you an example.

Every morning between seven and nine o'clock, into Times Square they roar: 28 Broadway local Number Ones; 20 Number Twos out of the Bronx; 19 Lexington Avenue Number Threes; 41 Flushing Number Sevens. Down Lexington Avenue into Grand Central Station: 25 Jerome Avenue Number Fives; 34 Pelham Avenue Number Sixes. Add up all the A, B, C, D through Q and R trains and 45 shut-tles, and we're talking about 130 route miles, 6,000 cars, 543 trains coming into the city every day. All told, some 3½ million riders a day. One-third of all mass transit users in the country. The largest sub-way system in the world. And know what? It was built by bonds. The tax-free bonds I sell.

"Do I believe this stuff? Am I for real? Do I even take the subway?" Of course I do, I'm a New Yorker. But there is a side of me that also likes to dig for worms, fish, catch fireflies, count the stars, pull off the road and pick the daisies, walk in the woods, talk to trees, cool my tootsies on mossy banks, skip rocks, lie down beside still waters, cup my hand and drink out of streams, watch the beaver, see an otter, see anything in the wild.

And that's the side of me that pitched camp in the North Woods of Wisconsin, imported otter pups to the site, filmed them growing up through four seasons, and produced *Flash, The Teenage Otter* for Walt Disney. Can you believe that this self-styled nature boy is also an evangelist for that mealymouthed word that sticks to the roof of the mouth like peanut butter on white bread: Infrastructure. Have passion, will travel.

> *People have got to see that a dollar spent on a school, highway, pump station is supermoney. You borrow at 6 percent. You improve the community at 7 percent. Paper money turns into productive assets that create jobs and incomes and real wealth. The end result is bridges that leap over obstacles to traffic and commerce, solid waste facilities that recycle our leftovers and turn them back into useful form, and mass transit that gets people to their jobs on time and home again, the richer for a day's work. Ah, productivity. I kneel at thy altar.*

Is this what you really want to do, Jim? Stump for subways and sewers, waterworks and wastewater treatment plants? When I graduated from Princeton in 1949 with a degree in political science, *Life* magazine gave me a startling choice of becoming a *Life* photographer or a *Life* writer.

For me, it was no contest. At 10 years of age, I owned a Voitlander camera, a Rolleiflex at age 12, a Speed Graphic at 15. As a 19-year-old, I had already sold *Life* a shot that made "picture of the week," a knothole gang of tennis fans on their bellies watching the U.S. Open. I had the eye. I had the credentials. I had the sensibilities of a photographer. And I had enough evidence in the D I got for this tortured translation of the story of Hercules and Cacus from Virgil's *Aeneid* to cut a wide swath around the written word for the rest of my life:

Hercules at the early dawn was aroused from his sleep. When he looked over with his eyes the herd and felt that part were missing from the number, he rushed to the nearest cave if by chance they were led themselves there by the tracks. When he saw all those tracks turned out of doors and did not see that some were carried in another direction, confused and uncertain in mind, he started to move at once from that cluttered place. Then when certain of the driven cattle lowed to the closed in cattle, the voice of the cattle turned Hercules around, longing for a return sound from the cave so that a cry of the concealed ones might be made. When Cacus had tried to keep him away by force, wandering toward the cave having been struck with a club, crying out to no one at all, he stretched out to meet the loyalty of the shepherd with death.

163

So which was it to be, writer or photographer? Riiiight! Writer! After all that education . . . what? Take pictures? Photography? Photography isn't work. It is fun. Writing is work, more like what a job should be. So listening to the left side of my brain—the no-fun, glutton-for-punishment side—of course, writer, orator, preacher it had to be:

Economists talk in billions and trillions. Makes the little guy feel like a bump on a log. Yet, no activity by individuals acting in their own self-interest has as much impact on the nation's well-being as saving. So, our company, together with the Dormitory Authority of the State of New York have done something about that. Tax-Free Munisavers and Tax-Free Beginner Bonds for families and individuals with only a thousand dollars or so to invest at a time.

A guy called the other day. "Saw your ad," he said. Put $1,000 in? Take $2,000 out? How do I get the thousand? The answer is: By someone else saving—and investing those savings in better tools of production that give rise to jobs, paychecks and savings for everybody.

We writerly dogs who have to look at the words we commit to paper are constantly being told "Bad dog!" by our own scold of a left brain. "Don't you ever feel guilty, Jimmy Lebenthal, for taking bread, all that tax-free income, out of the Treasury's mouth?" A little. But I know *the* one reason individual retail investors buy the bonds of towns they have never heard of, or have heard all too much about, is because the interest is tax-free. As a matter of fact, I have always figured Lebenthal actually saves everybody money as taxpayers by helping the mayors and governors borrow for public necessities at low rates of interest in the tax-free bond market. (I once told Senator Al D'Amato that I'd sooner go back to Disney and paint the assholes out of chipmunks, than sell taxable municipal bonds.) And now, helping myself freely to the best description of what a municipal bond man does for a living from Edward N. Luttwak's *Endangered American Dream* (Simon & Schuster, 1994), and with a touch of the politician's singsong in my voice, I went into my windup on rebuilding America with tax-free municipal bonds:

As a fellow bond wonk, my job is to convert America's rivulets of savings into those rivers of longer-term investments. Through the saving-investing, borrowing-lending process, people's unspent income turns into schools, training facilities, factories, housing, roads, airports—tools of production that create real wealth and pay off in benefits for generations to come.

The federal government doesn't have to twist itself into a pretzel trying to invent some new form of tax-free savings bond. The bonds of our great American cities and states—your bonds, Mr. Mayor, Madam Mayor—are already tax-free. They are the only tool we've got for rebuilding America and getting this magnificent country off its magnificent bottom. Munis are too good for the rich alone. And that is why I want to turn Americans into savers. And savers into buyers of your bonds.

My written speech was in my pocket and it stayed there. Because standing up there on a stage in Portland with all those mayoral ears to be bent, I suddenly realized I was in my element. Freed from the tyranny of my nemesis, the written word, everything I was meant to be came out in the convincing spontaneity of the spoken word. Who was that guy up there? It was me, Jim "Built by Bonds" Lebenthal. And you can write that down.

LEBENTHAL TO GO

No matter how humdrum your job
and your life, think of your story
as spilling the beans.
Now you've got their attention.
What makes a good story?
Details that advance the plot.
Being kidnapped is interesting.
Being kidnapped by gypsies and
sold to your parents is fascinating.

If you think about it for a minute,
your life—yes, yours—
would make a great movie.
Possibly X-rated.

166

11

By Everything Possessed

Impossible Not to Love

She was the one who called me, "The Real James Bond."

She said that was because I hounded senatorial aides, mayors, citizens, even as I evangelized us bond sellers in my "one-man crusade" to save the munis from the federal government's proposal to tax them.

She also wrote, "Lebenthal doesn't balance the books or do other 'adult' things. He is the family firm's self-proclaimed spiritual leader . . . a preeminent spieler with a country preacher's command of theatrics . . . he is by turns, a curmudgeon, good shepherd and aggrieved bene-factor of his flock. . . ."

Back in 1985, Bernice Kanner, my coauthor, sized me up and summed me up in *New York Magazine* this way:

At Lebenthal & Company, the prodigal son is thought of as a blend of inspiring and exasperating. "Jim makes a wonderful contribution," says his sister, Eleanor Bissinger, who is 15 months older. "But he is a source of untold frustration. If there's ever a foul-up, you just know Jim is behind it in some way. . . . Jim will deploy our messengers—bonds be damned—for some trivial mission," she continues. "You might call him upending. He has one of the finest senses of humor in the world, and I love him, but most of the time I'm angry with him. . . . Wherever he is, a trail of bedlam follows." Lebenthal labels his sister a martinet, but adds, "Gerry and Eleanor work their asses off and all they ever hear is How wonderful Jim was on TV." It's a scene from *Joseph and His Coat of Many Colors.*

That's fine for as far as the eye can see of a character who acts like he's his own boss and has to go his own way. But what the eye never can see is that Great Ideas have a life all their own. So, when I'm "Present at the Creation" and feel the whammy and the electrons orbit inside my head, it means that the idea owns me. When I turn an elusive, abstract idea into a concrete image making it my "Art," that truly makes it my thing. But you can't own Great Ideas. They own you. And boy, have I been owned and driven by some beauties—ideas that, for all my odd, freewheeling, rambunctious behavior, have added a little something to everybody's happiness.

I Don't Swim in Your Finger Bowls. So Not in My River You Don't!

In the spirit of making the environment cleaner and the earth a better place, I took a piece of graffiti and turned it into the war cry for a high quality, triple-A issuer of municipal bonds. Let me tell you how and why.

The New York State Environmental Facilities Corporation was issuing a new kind of bond for bringing the state's wastewater treatment plants up to snuff. These new bonds would be backed by a slew of safety features, any one of which would have made the bonds a conservative investment. First, the bonds were backed by the general obligation bonds (GOs) secured by the taxing power of a whole pool of municipalities. As they say in the Passover song, *Dayenu* (It would be enough). At least one-third of the money to repay the bonds was already on hand in a federal and state-financed reserve fund. *Dayenu!* Then, that fund's earnings subsidized the interest that the municipalities had to pay on their GOs, making their bonds all that easier to pay. *Dayenu,* again! Finally, as an extra club over its head, state aid would be withheld from any municipality if it missed a debt service payment. *Dayenu!* You bet, enough for a triple-A.

There was a big problem, and it had nothing to do with safety. The name of the bonds was 14 words long: New York State Environmental Facilities Corporation Water Pollution Control State Revolving Fund Revenue Bonds (14, count 'em! 14). The only surefire way I knew to get that tongue twister into the investor's head was to create a fish that I named the "Last Angry Trout." I taught that trout to say (when I spoke on its behalf), "New York State Environmental Facilities Corporation State Revolving Fund Water Pollution Control Revenue Bonds." So on Earth Day in 1990, I got on radio and read the Last Angry Trout's warning: "Stop dumping in our rivers and streams. I don't swim in your fingerbowls. So not in my river you don't."

Yes, you know and I know that nobody buys bonds out of love for the good ol' hometown wastewater treatment plant. A bond's purpose is the last thing on the investor's mind. It is the wallet issues that count: coupon, price, and yield. And even then, you've got to break through the clutter to make people stand still and listen. My Last Angry Trout opened ears to a sales pitch you'd listen to coming *only* from a fish and turned sewers and wastewater treatment plants into—well—fun. How'd the deal go? Why, swimmingly. People were delighted and called for more information about those "Last Angry Trout" bonds. And the Lebenthal brokers sold them hand . . . over fish.

Where do great ideas come from, anyway? After enough brooding and mulling, some of my best ideas for our Lebenthal Friday newsletters have come to me that morning in the shower, or on the subway. I got my best headline on municipal bond insurance, "You Will Be Paid," hurtling uptown between Union Square and Grand Central on the Number 4 subway. The impetus for "The Short Course In Municipal Bonds for People Who Think Savings Belong in a Bank" happened in front of the Guggenheim Museum. I invented the Lebenthal Bond Exchange (for working out tax swaps) in the dentist's chair. "It's like 7 percent from a Bank" dawned on me between beers at a bar. And showing the "bid" price that we'd pay you right alongside our "ask" price if you were selling the bonds back to us, was triggered when a Rollerblader zipped by on Park Avenue.

My favorite place to receive messages-from-within is the literati-studded Manhattan restaurant, Elaine's. I go there alone and sit at a deceptively undesirable little table opposite the kitchen, and wait for the arrival of the muse. Sure enough, I got the idea for this book, when I was stirred, not shaken, by a martini and half bottle of Pinot Grigio.

The idea for the Last Angry Trout was something else again. Frankly, I stole it from graffiti in a Princeton men's room. It was Ivy League graffiti: "I don't piss in your ashtrays, so don't throw butts in this urinal." At the Decorator's Club, the oldest women's professional club in America (of which my wife Jackie was president), some of the grandest dames of interior design still call me "Mr. Trout." Little do they know where my inspiration came from.

How Does a Guy like Me Get a Wife like My Jackie?

Have you ever seen a couple and asked yourself, "What in the world did she see in him?" I even ask myself, "How did I ever get my Jackie?" Luckily enough, I met Jackie Beymer by hiring her as my interior decorator, *before* joining Lebenthal & Company. After all, how romantic and appealing to a girl is a guy who sells municipal bonds for his mother?

I have always loved Jackie's type. And who wouldn't? Soft, kind, luscious, full-lipped, blonde, blue-eyed outdoorsy beauties, whose gorgeous faces, usually framed by a Stetson or floppy beach hat, just have to be kissed. Our daughter Claudia captured it nicely when she wrote in *Allure* magazine (April 2003), "I have always had a beautiful mother, equally chic in a Chanel suit as in Wrangler Jeans . . . and my father has always had a beautiful wife."

Jackie was a true girl of the Golden West, hailing from Twin Falls, Idaho. As a matter of fact, Jackie was the first girl from Idaho to go to Vassar. When we met, I was an advertising hotshot, a copywriter at Young & Rubicam. She lifted an eyebrow at my obsession with Chef Boyardee Ravioli and Goodyear "3-T Triple Tempered Nylon Cord." But, for purposes of "product research," Jackie went along with me, and let Life Savers melt down to nothing on her tongue, just to see how long they'd last. She also let me wash her hair to prove Johnson & Johnson's "No Tears, No Tangles" baby shampoo really worked.

Jackie had always gone for slightly wacky guys in high school. But when it came to decorating my apartment, I gave her such a hard time, constantly plugging my own ideas, we both swore we'd never go through that again with another person. So, instead we got married.

I think Bernice got it right in "The Real James Bond" article (*New York Magazine,* March 24, 1986) when she said:

It was Lebenthal's zany antics that won his wife. He'd call constantly with decorating schemes. One day saying he'd found a shoeshine chair that would make a terrific lamp. Another day that he'd found a post office screen that would make a divine room divider. Once, he called chagrined. He and an artist friend had painted a huge, tacky Venice-scene mural on one wall. Of course, it had to be painted over, but it shows Jim's enthusiasms.

So that's my Jackie: dreamboat, glamour puss, scholar, globe-trotter, interior decorator, organization lady, and creator of her *Look-It-Up-Book,* "always a place for everything and everything in its place." And everything in life was idyllic, until slowly, barely noticeably, little things changed, things were forgotten, things were misplaced: My life mate, helpmate, soul mate Jackie has Alzheimer's.

Friends ask me when I saw the first signs, when I first noticed. I look for clues, going as far back as the faraway look in our honeymoon photographs, or each time she took the exam to get into the stage design union and failed, or (with the test of anyone's strength and fortitude) her total redoing of our kitchen.

Now I wonder how many things around the house, unexplained incidents, early traits, even her singular virtues that I once chalked up to her unique personality, were the earliest stirrings of a disease for which there exists no kinder word than dementia?

Jackie manifested a fanaticism about organization:

In her filing system that had more pigeonholes than there could possibly be subjects to shove into them.

In her linen closet with every sheet secure in its own plastic holder.

In her *Look It Up Book,* a precursor to Filofax, for helping working mothers keep everything in one place so they could run their household from the office. It was a superb volume, from which she derived only mortification and self-rebuke, once she realized that a "hickey," a tiny speck of dust on one page of the plates where the ink hadn't hit, would appear in all 5,000 copies.

Even in Jackie the Interior Decorator's quarter-million-dollar redo of our kitchen with its two dishwashers, two ovens, two of everything, one for "roast" and one for "toast."

In our fight over the can of crabmeat she snatched out of my hand in a desperate state because she couldn't get the words out fast enough, "I'm saving that for crab-cakes for dinner tomorrow night."

When the images of our 45 years of marriage come to mind, they always have tags on them, like courtroom evidence, Exhibit A, Exhibit B. . . . Not as submissions in evidence of her Jackiness, but as signs of a dear and creative, organized and aesthetic, soft-spoken woman slowly taking leave of her memories and identity and turning into a damned and tormented soul.

This articulate conversationalist can no longer speak. This inventive cook can no longer feed herself. Or change TV channels. Or even get up from a chair.

But in a striking reversal of the Lord giveth and the Lord taketh away, the Lord hath given. Into our lives, he has sent Maria Canosa, a present-day miracle worker playing the Annie Sullivan role to Jackie's Helen Keller.

Maria has turned Jackie back into a globe-trotter. They live in Costa Rica. Earlier in Jackie's Alzheimer's, Maria had taken Jackie to San Jose, Maria's hometown in Costa Rica. They stayed a blissful month in Maria's daughter Giorgianella's lively, family-filled house. But once back in New York, Jackie writhed in anxiety and squirmed out of any chair she was sitting in and slumped to the floor. It seemed so obvious. "Maria, you and Jackie go back to Costa Rica!" "We can't," Maria said, "Giorgia's getting divorced and the house is being sold."

No problem. I simply bought the house. It is a house that, in Yonkers, would be a castle for a family with kids. Only it's in Costa Rica, and it is filled with Maria's embracing nieces, nephews, sisters, and in-laws, coming and going and filling Jackie's life with action.

Does Jackie recognize me when I visit? Does she know where she is and what is going on around her? But those are not the right questions. Jackie is not there to entertain us. It is we who are there to show some regard for life. Amazingly, owing to some wonderful secretion that nourishes the traveler's soul, Jackie appears blessed with contentment as long as visitors are around—or as long as she and Maria are on the go. Jackie can be lifted out of a recliner, piled into an

SUV, wheeled everywhere, and transported like one of those festival saints carried on the villagers' shoulders, only instead of to the village square during *Carnevale,* it is to the mall in a very human tribute to activity and life.

Thank you, Maria, for helping Jackie, and all the rest of us, to go on living.

I'm the Man Who Found the Only Word That Rhymes with Orange

In Dad's home movies, I swim frantically, apparently without breathing. My arms are windmilling. My face is in the water. The scene ends with telltale perforation marks at the end of the roll. Dad runs out of film before I ever come up for air. That is the story of my life: Commit wholeheartedly to whatever I do, with all my body and soul, might and mane. Breathe afterward.

At Young & Rubicam, I was assigned to think up the first commercial introducing the new powerful Excedrin to the world. I'll be damned if I was going to walk into Charlie Feldman, the copy chief's office, with still another slice-of-life commercial, and frame-by-frame storyboard of headache pain. Not me! I walked in with a gargantuan blowup of the mother of headaches: a mug shot of U.S. Air Force rocket sled test pilot, Colonel John Paul Stapp. In the shot, 652 MPH sonic winds and 35 times the pull of gravity pin the good colonel's ears, eyes, nose, and throat to the back of his head. "Now, Charlie, there's an Excedrin Headache for you!" My brainstorm never saw the light of day. "My god, Jim. It's only a headache remedy," Feldman scowled. "It's not supposed to be a cure for cancer." Alright, I'd get my jollies by applying my genius somewhere else. And the "somewhere else" turned out to be Princeton University.

Years ago, a classmate asked me to join him in a Princeton Annual Giving Telethon. Princeton has perfected the art of using alums to solicit other alums for money: gifts from the heart, with no strings attached for whatever Princeton needs. The university raises $37 million a year from 60 percent of the alumni, a full 10 percent of its operating budget, through the persistence of guys like me hammering away at classmates on the telephone or in the U.S. mail. I was a sledge hammer for the Class of 1949 ("All for One, One Four Nine!"). "Jim, I appreciate what you're doing," classmates who were jokers and cutups in our school days, would pull a face and say. "But dammit, Jim, No! I don't like the way the university is going."

I wonder, why can't I take no for an answer? I mean, I certainly know why I can't if I'm talking to a bond prospect who I know is loaded with dough and truly belongs in munis. Because that guy is going to end up buying. And since I've done all the hard work softening him up, I don't want him to buy from somebody else.

But I was intrigued by the earful of reasons my classmates gave me for *not* giving to Princeton and, frankly, it embarrassed me a little. These holdouts seemed to know something I didn't know about the place. So I literally went back to school to learn what they knew so I could do the same thing for Princeton that I do when I advertise munis for Lebenthal. Find the button that trumps logic, strikes a nerve—and then, push it!

It took 10 years of nonstop letter writing and button pushing, but I lifted the Class of 1949 off its ample bottom in Annual Giving and raised it to, well, average in dollars and participation. But I did it in a most unaverage way. Stuff that could have been treated like junk mail, I made good-natured entertainment and fun.

Once I told my brethren that, going through Princeton without giving to Annual Giving was like going through life skipping dessert:

Dear Classmate:

How's your wife, your ticker, your TV reception? All pretty good? Then read no more, because there's nothing here for you. I'm only offering what you've already got plenty of: happiness. The happiness of snow replaced by dogwoods on a glorious spring day. Rockets going off in class. Eureka! Learning something you simply never dreamed of before. Skimming old "78" records across the courtyard. (This was before anybody thought of inventing the Frisbee.) The grass freshly cut, the infield newly graded, being first out for practice on a crisp day. Thud! The surprise to the kidneys, when it got another love letter from the wonderful world of contact sports.

Without a scintilla of logic, I told my classmates, "It feels good. It warms the heart. It replenishes. It restores the soul. It waters the roots. It keeps the memory green. It reverses ill will. It aids forgiving and forgetting. It swells the chest. It straightens the spine. It fills the shoes of givers past." I did go on and make one concession to reason. I acknowledged that giving to Princeton does save on taxes.

In another appeal, I warned of the dangers of *not giving.* If allowed to go unchecked too long, not giving can become a macabre cause in itself. The search for self-justification in not giving can lead to ill humor, anomie, miasma, and worse, the "Princeton Disconnection," evidenced by the dreaded postgraduate syndrome of cold heart, dry eyes, and no pulse.

I expanded on what I meant. The Princeton Disconnection amounts to wearing orange and black as a color combination and not as a statement. It means turning the radio to another station during the football scores without waiting for the results of the Princeton game. It occurs when somebody says, "tiger," in the game of Free Association, and you come up with the word "zoo" instead of beaming "Princeton." It can find you being introduced to another Princetonian and not asking, "What Class?" And not even trying to fake the words to "Old Nassau" anymore. Worst of all, it's tossing out this letter in its envelope, unopened, with the junk mail.

I grabbed lapels and twisted arms, but I never, never told a classmate how much to give. My goal was participation. But compelling as the heart might be, no class with over 100 living members has ever had 100 percent participation in Annual Giving. So I started a chain letter, a postal posse to get William R. Alley Jr., the first guy in the class whose name began with "A" to harangue the next in line.

I told the "A's" and the "Bs" through "Z" that they needn't be bighearted, rah-rah, or even rich to join the club. They just had to have sat in class next to others in the great chain of giving—Jackson, Jacob, Jacobeen, Jacobson, Jadwin, Jamieson, Jarrell, Jenks, Jennings, and Jessup. (The "J's" represented the longest sequence of names in alphabetical order of classmates who'd given the year before in the annual drive.)

It's uncanny how gifts come in these runs, I mused. What is it about Jackson through Jessup, or Leibert, Leiper, Lennan, Levine, Ling, Lingua, Lipinski, London (the next longest list of givers) that immunizes these guys against the Princeton Disconnection?

Explain the chemistry that alkalizes the resistance of Remington, Rentshcler, Repp, Reynolds, Rheinstein, Richardson, and Riddle, to sitting down and writing out a check, or that pulls so powerfully at the purse and heartstrings of Huber, Huber, Hughes, Hughes, Hughes, and Hungerford. What do Dickenson, Dickson, Diehl, Dignan, Dingwall, Doak drink that kills the pain and heals the wounds of change?

While Dr. Gary Oehlert, assistant professor of statistics in the math department, called these runs of magnanimity typical Markov chains, I said, "No!" It all came down to whom you sat next to. And I pointed out that there was more than chance at work here. In fact, I offered my classmates an incentive at least to go for the impossible of 100 percent participation: a symbol of the impossible. A rhyme for the word orange. I promised each member of the longest chain of givers in alphabetical sequence a priceless Princeton relic, a genuine door hinge from an old dorm, a door hinge painted orange. It became the coveted Class of 1949 Orange Door Hinge. (Now, Dear Reader, your objection that orange and door hinge don't rhyme is overruled! I sent my comely assistant to an audio laboratory to record her rhyming the two words, and bring back a voice print. Oscillographs don't lie. The match up of her reading is indisputable. "Oringe doringe rhymes!" The first and only rhyme for that glorious orb in the sky.)

A Fly, a Strikeout, a Run

I can always tell when I'm about to be possessed by a Great Idea. The glow in the dark, as Tinker Bell descends from the rafters, the resonance of Great Ideas going "boinggg!" Boinggg is no guarantee of future success. It just means another "At Bat" with every intention of slugging the ball out of the park. But you learn something even when you strike out. If you don't, as Santayana tells us, you are doomed to repeat your failures.

Even as I write this advice, I'm reminded that I almost repeated a mistake that I made 50 years ago in the control booth at KFSD-TV, San Diego. I was directing a live commercial for a local used car dealer. In the rehearsal, I could not believe what I saw on the monitor: The dealer's highly polished automobiles were parading past the camera in a crass, vulgar display of bad taste. Each one of those secondhand cars had the price in the windshield, a gaudy card

181

that filled the screen as the cars drove by. I shouted into the headset of the assistant director out in the car lot, "Get those price cards out of there." I must say, it improved the shot. Unfortunately, it left nothing to indicate that the cars might be a good buy. The car dealer got a free commercial. Make-Good for him. Strike-Out out for me.

What's that got to do with this book? Only this: For an instant, I had the urge to yank the pithy "Lebenthal To Go" sections at the end of each one of these chapters, which take these nice, polished stories and reduce them to one-liners. But, those who forget the past are doomed to repeat it. So the "Lebenthal To Go" sections stay. Read, heed, and enjoy them.

Here's a nice curve ball I recently popped up, up, and away and then dropped into the centerfielder's mitt. I'm talking about the saga of our 30-minute Infomercial, "How to Buy Municipal Bonds on TV with Jim Lebenthal." First, you must understand, leads are our bread and butter. Because selling municipal bonds is not a churning business. Our customers buy to hold, and we may not see that money again for another 5, 10, 20 years. So we constantly need "fresh blood," ad leads, lots of them, since only one out of ten are ever likely to develop into actual bond-buying customers. I could not watch successful infomercials for the Ginzu Knife, Rotato Potato Peeler, or Ronco Rotisserie ("Set it and forget it!") without thinking, "What a dramatic way to teach a mass audience about the heady joys of tax-free income, get leads, maybe lots of leads, and really hit the jackpot." So, my colleagues went along and let me produce a lively, information-packed Infomercial. We rewired all the telephones in the office to bypass any possible bottleneck at the switchboard and let the brokers handle the expected onslaught of incoming calls, with a cheerful, "Hello, this is Lebenthal!" We bought a half hour on local TV, stood by, and counted down, Five seconds . . . four . . . three . . . two . . . one. You're on the air!

This story does not turn out the way you think. Oh, the telephones did ring like crazy: over 2,000 calls in one half hour and for several minutes after. And 2,000 Lebenthal Bond Kits—with listings of our latest offerings of bonds that we had for sale—went out to 2,000 newcomers who had simply never had the impulse to think about municipal bonds, let alone call a broker. For an excellent reason. They had no money. They did not belong in a market where the initial investment is usually $25,000 or so. It felt wonderful to be at bat and see the ball soar. I mean 2,000 leads in a half hour was truly "knocking the cover off the ball." But I had popped the pitch to 2,000 unqualified curiosity seekers. "Hello, this is Lebenthal!" was sung out 2,000 times. But you could fit the leads we converted in your eye.

I want to turn Americans into savers. And then I do want to turn them into buyers of municipal bonds. But it takes money to save. And to have enough left over (after you have paid the butcher, the baker, the candlestick maker) to plunk down $25,000 for municipal bonds. I must commend my associates at Lebenthal & Company for letting me try. I told myself, "I don't have to do that again." Or do I?

Yes, I do. I am compelled to listen to a good idea, thence go where it takes me. The next time up, I hit a grand slam. So, let me tell you about my home run, the MuniProfiler.

The MuniProfiler is actually me, Jim Lebenthal, in a "box," doing just what I've done in the flesh or on the phone for 42 years: listening, analyzing, and advising people, and matching them up with bonds tailored to their needs. The MuniProfiler is a mathematical model of the decisions I make with customers. At the turn of the millennium (in the year 2000), I had myself modeled into the MuniProfiler, a software program on our web site that does, guess what? It listens, analyzes, and advises people and matches them up with bonds tailored to their needs. And I called it the MuniProfiler. It does everything I do, without the beady stare of the salesman in me beating you into submission to buy. And it never grows inattentive, never grows bored, never tires of creating alternate portfolios for each very different investor.

While sitting at home, anyone with a computer can log onto www.lebenthal.com and click MuniProfiler. Up pops a questionnaire with all the questions I would ask you: your age, income, amount to invest, investment objectives, your attitude about risk, when you want to see your money come back, your willingness to reach for yield by extending maturity, and your willingness to defer your interest to the date your bonds finally mature. After you fill it out at your own pace, hit submit. And within seconds, up pops a portfolio of real bonds that are actually for sale and that match your answers. Of course, just on the odd chance that you may want to buy them, or get more information, up pops the face and voice of someone at Lebenthal you can talk to, when you are good and ready.

The MuniProfiler is how municipal bonds are going to be sold in the twenty-first century. Why do I say so? Because the MuniProfiler gets hits all day, 24/7, from people who could never quite bring themselves to pick up the telephone and call. Oh, sure, some of them are just window-shopping. Some even have fun adjusting their answers and bringing up different combinations of coupon, yield, and maturity. But some of those window-shoppers actually become customers and buy bonds. Admittedly, the conversion ratio is low, compared with a live investor walking in and sitting down with a broker. But who cares about conversion rates, when it costs the MuniProfiler only the price of a zap of electricity to scan our inventory when all our bonds are posted on our web site anyway? Give me a 1 percent conversion rate all day long. The way I see it, all it takes to make money is for one person to walk into Tiffany's and say, "I'll take the diamond tiara . . . it caught my eye in your window."

Egged on by One Smile and 20,000 Go-Sign Men

I have always followed my bliss, pursuing my own little world with heart and soul. That's why I took on crisis after crisis like New York's fiscal crisis, the Social Security tax on municipal bonds, the 1986 Tax Reform Act, and relished turning them all into personal fires I could go running to and try putting out. But when was I going to make good on a certain other pledge that haunted me?

Once, years ago, while writhing in agony I promised God that if He would stop my killer migraines triggered by a spinal tap. . . . I would make *Children's Movies.* God did stop the pain. The second I swore my oath.

But alas, while 10 years raced by, I did nothing about keeping my vow. . . . I thought, I better check to see if the Almighty is still holding me to it. This time the test was more mundane; a broken radio that hadn't worked in an age. If God would turn it on, I would make more *T-Is-For-Tumbleweed* type movies for kids. Well, I turned the knob. The radio started right up with Vaughn Monroe singing *Racing with the Moon.* So, there you are! I still owed God some movies that were clean and rated G for the whole family.

All that was a long time ago. And here I was on September 11, 2001, still at Lebenthal, mother now gone and daughter Alexandra in total command, the third generation of Lebenthals to run the company. I was getting ready to pay my debt to God at last, when it happened! Not only the destruction of *the* Twin Towers, but the destruction of *my* Twin Towers.

Back in 1991, I produced a television commercial with tourists strolling about the pair of hulking superstructures, all reflected against a woman's mirrored sunglasses. "Sure, it could be shorter or fatter or curvier," my voice over monologue began. "But you've got to love what it does. Draws 60,000 workers a day to paying jobs right here in the Port of New York and New Jersey and sends them home at night, the richer for a day's work. You see the twin towers of the World Trade Center. I see two giant economic pumps built by the tax-free bonds I sell." Then I appeared magnified to 100 stories tall, superimposed between the towers. "I'm Jim Lebenthal," I declared. "Love my towers. Love my bonds."

Lebenthal's office is only 1,000 feet away from Ground Zero. The morning of 9/11, I joined the hoards escaping the devastation. Reaching Church Street and Chambers, I turned back and looked hard at the horror, just before the buildings fell. I remember thinking how the blizzard of paper, backlit by the sun, flew and fluttered out of the burning upper floors, looking like a Broadway ticker tape parade. And I quickly thought, "Wait a minute. Steel melts!" As if on cue, first one tower, then the other imploded and sank in painful slow motion to the earth. They replaced themselves with thick, towering black cumulous clouds of dust and debris bearing down on the heels of humanity desperately racing to get out of the way.

Like everybody right after 9/11, I wondered, would we ever smile again? I thought not . . . until I came upon one of the hundreds of color photocopies of missing victims, turning fences into shrines all over Manhattan. This photograph in Union Square Park was of a young woman who had worked in one of the high floors in the second tower. I sat for an hour watching as passersby stopped to smile back at her and read the tribute her family had posted,

"Marina Gertzberg, 25, and Always Smiling." That smile, that manifestation of life, talked directly to me and purged me of my 9/11 depression:

"Time's up, Jim. Time to let the artist in you out, and make those little movies you promised God, Jim."

Prodded by Marina Gertzberg's invigorating smile and also egged on by the new Go-Man signs, flashing and nagging at me from 20,000 traffic lights all around New York City, "Do it, Jim. Just Do it! And make good on your pledge, Jim!"—I finally did. I finally turned the guy in the business suit, who had once spurned becoming a *Life* photographer, back into someone with an eye, a nose, and a camera, a street reporter for www.crazyaboutnewyork.com, my own personal web site.

I've kept the business suit on. And I still beat the drum and rattle the tambourine for New York City bonds. But in the cloak of night, or glare of day, I go around the city and poke into its heart, soul, and *ribs.* I am ready to pounce, with my Sony MiniDigital camera, on the unseen—unseen because it is right under your nose—and bring it right up there in front of your eyes.

I am doing for all New York City what I once did only for its bonds. I am taking the ordinary, the plain, and the commonplace wherever I find them in this crazy, wonderful, mixed up goulash of a city and bringing them to life on www.crazyaboutnewyork.com. The opportunity for fun and entertainment is everywhere in this *"town that has no ceiling price, the town of double-talk, the town so big men named it twice—like so, N'Yawk/N'Yawk"* (Christopher Morley).

I see (and shoot) the joke in all those windblown plastic bags tossed and stuck in the limbs of the trees along Broadway and instead of muttering "How ugly!" my video transforms them, as they undulate to the strains of the Sons of the Pioneers singing "Tumbling Tumbleweeds."

With my trusty camera, I turn the scourge of the ubiquitous cell phone into the voice of the poet. The "poet" is me reciting Walt Whitman's "Leaves of Grass" into my cell phone and making it seem to come out of the cell phone and (uninvited) into the ear of everybody else on their cell phones.

I zoom in on the source of that elusive "Tweet, tweet, tweeting," heard even in the thick and din of city traffic, and reveal the secret hideaway of the sparrows who hatch their young in the crossbars that hold up New York City's street lights.

There's a street person I call the Lens Hog. His game is ruining tourist's snapshots of George Washington on Wall Street by inserting himself into the picture. I caught all the fun of his maddening skill in my camera by deliberately letting him "ruin" my shots of George from this angle and that, and with music turn his caper into a Bugs Bunny-like routine.

It is all grist for my mill: tumbleweeds, municipal bonds, and the crazyaboutnewyork love letters on my web site. They're all just excuses for me to walk down Broadway, see the *life* in whatever exists and by turning the ordinary into art make you see the spectacle of the Great What Is, through laughing, loving eyes.

If Paderewski Could, Then so Could I

Have I made it sound like I was managing the noble House of Lebenthal on my own, perhaps with benign neglect? Not so. The company's president and leader for 20 years was my sister Eleanor's husband, H. Gerard Bissinger. Eleanor ran daily operations. Gerry ran trading, sales, and everything else with an occasional flared nostril and a top kick's command but stingless humor that made it fun to be the butt of his brusque repartee. You said you wouldn't touch something for all the tea in China. He said, "Wish I'd said that." You said someone's a crude, uncouth Philistine. He said, "Yeah, but with a little more polish, he'd be a diamond in the rough." You said you hated *Tree of the Wooden Clogs* with every bone in your body, Gerry said, "Can I put you down as doubtful?" You said to him in his hospital bed, "How are you feeling, Gere?" He said, "I just came out of chemo. And the rest is history."

Bissinger was a chunky, funny, masculine, feared, revered leaderly ex-Marine and former advertising account man with a passion for numbers and strong analytical mind. The perfect complement to my free spirit. Between the two of us, with his orderly, rational left brain and my free wheeling, spontaneous right brain—the half I fly by the seat of the pants with, the half my creative ideas come from, the half that tells my heart, "Do it! Just do it, do it, do it"—we made an art of selling municipal bonds to the retail investor and Lebenthal a shining landmark on the business skyline of New York City. When you make your job your art, you make it your own.

And then came this memo from Eleanor and Gerry:

> About 9 months ago we told you that we intend to retire within 3 years. Frankly, we are ready to retire today, but do not think that would be fair to you or the company . . . you should totally involve yourself in all major decisions such as the additional (office) space and the selection of personnel to take over our functions. For example, current operations. You must make sure you understand how we currently operate; what our current economic position is; how a change in our economic position affects our operations, or our ability to operate. For example, the cost of occupying the additional space will reduce our net capital and thereby the number of bonds we can carry. . . .

Did El and Gerry take early retirement because they felt they made the money and I spent it? Was it because they did the work and I got the recognition? Was it because mothers are nicer to their sons than to their daughters and their daughters' husbands?

All of the above, and I had to face the reality that my sister and brother-in-law were retiring, leaving me with the ranch, and that I'd better learn what Gerry meant when he wrote, "the cost of occupying the additional space will reduce our net capital and thereby the number of bonds we can carry."

I'd show 'em. If the concert pianist Paderewski could make it as the prime minister of Poland, I could make it as the FINOP (the Financial and Operations Principal) of Lebenthal—a license, if there ever was one, to run a municipal bond business. So, one fine day, I hired a trainer. For 30 days, I boned up for the NASD's six-hour Series 27 FINOP exam. I took it. I passed it. And today, I am a certifiably whole person with both sides of a human brain, left and right. I have the papers to prove it: my Series 27 license.

LEBENTHAL TO GO

Everybody has a tie to someone
with Alzheimer's.
Don't worry about whether your
mom recognizes you. The important thing is
that you still recognize her.

Hate the way life changes so fast?
Don't take it out on your Alma Mater!

How can you take advantage
of the impersonal wonders of the
Internet and still add the value
of your personal touch?
That's the challenge for any salesperson today.

Just for the fun of it, let your
own inner artist out. It might just
improve your job performance.

You can be a good manager, too.
Management is nothing more than
organized common sense.

My spin on "find a job you like
and you won't work a day in your life"
is "find a job you love, and you'll
work at it until you drop."

12

What Happened When Money Dropped in the Preacher's Lap?

Because Life's Been Good . . . So Far

Two years ago, he was stung by a bee. His immune system had been shot through by the medicine he was taking for Parkinson's, and within moments, he was dead. And while his family wasn't exactly poor, even $2.6 million doesn't go far these days, not even for a widow who watches the pennies and has never even owned a shearling. But suppose she wanted one, or a mink, or wanted to help the kids, $10,000 here, $10,000 there, or redo the kitchen? Could she afford to live as worry-free as she had? And what if she lived forever, with no letup in outlays for the house, taxes, gas, phone, and electricity, and don't forget inflation and life's expensive little surprises that would never let up.

The plucky widow's way of planning for tomorrow was to take up committee work, master the art of the painted wood finish, and to research the contribution of camp followers to the morale of both sides of the Revolutionary War. She would do anything but face the music and hunker down to the business of serious financial planning.

But look at who's talking. While I'm the pro who dishes out plenty of advice to others about getting their finances in order, I've done my share of procrastination by crucial pencil sharpening . . . then making sure all the hangers face the same way . . . polishing the silver . . . in short anything to avoid sitting down and facing up to deciding what I want out of life, and how to make sure I'm going to get it.

"So, where's my long-term-care insurance?" you ask. Oh, that! Well, I don't have any. That's why my wife Jackie and I are now both uninsurable. I often ponder how much that inattention to detail years ago will end up costing us down the road.

When I do think about it, how could I let two such un-threatening words—"financial" and "planning" keep me so long from practicing what I preach? How? Because I'm human. Because financial planning inevitably raises questions of one's own mortality. How long do I really think I'm going to live? After I'm gone, how much will it cost Jackie to live? Where is the money going to come from in sickness and health? From interest? From principal? How long can that last? What will be left for the kids? Do I really have as much as I think? What about my big dreams for retirement:

making children's movies, supporting Princeton and the Museum of the City of New York, buying a farm and plowing it by horse?

Knowing the digging, self-discipline, and soul baring (if only to yourself) that financial planning involves, naturally I took my sweet time getting around to it. So, what goaded me to finally step into a Lebenthal conference room and face the music? I'll tell you what. I needed a new commercial for Alexandra on financial planning at Lebenthal. That meant trekking up to my familiar haunt Elaine's restaurant with my ad guru, Ron Holland, to cook one up. Why Elaine's? I go there for poetic inspiration, from the ghosts of famous customers past floating around in the rafters, like Arthur Miller, Irwin Shaw, Irving Stone. Lifting up our eyes, Ron and I asked in the name of heaven, "Why does anyone need financial planning?" And in a flash, came the answer from the creative spirit haunting Elaine's, "Because life's been good . . . so far."

That provocative warning meant for the Lebenthal customer made Lebenthal himself think twice. How long could a good thing last? Better find out. Better make a plan. Heck, all it involves is going through a mountain of personal records and figuring out the rest of your life— and beyond. (Mustn't forget those heirs.)

Exposing the truth about my personal finances would cause librarians to yank this book off the shelf you found it on and hide it on the Medical Shelf under "Neurotics (Money)." Because even though making money on Wall Street is the daily topic, I seem to come up short on what it takes to rake it in. Too often, when I was selling a bond, I'd find myself cutting price and giving profits away. If I was shopping for a Christmas tree from one of those horse traders on Broadway, you'd find me bargaining the guy up. My salary at Lebenthal, $250,000 a year, wasn't chopped liver. But by Wall Street standards, nothing to shout about. That's okay, I figured that by running those ads and building the brand, I'd get my reward . . . in heaven. Whenever!

While we're at it, how much do you think a municipal bond firm should spend on advertising? Truthfully, it *should* spend nothing. You could do this business from the locker room of a golf club, or with branches at street level and walk-ins the way Merrill Lynch does. So what did I do? I resigned from my country club (after I got married and the dues went up). And I fought against branches and the fixed costs of all those desks and leases. Instead I spent $2,000,000 a year (20 percent of our operating budget!) on advertising. And my standard answer to anyone who asked, "How much is Lebenthal's advertising budget?" was the look on my face, "What do you mean? We don't have one." And we didn't until Advest, Inc. bought us and daughter Alexandra began coming clean on our media bills to the new owner in Hartford.

So, up to the sale, I owned no portfolio of municipal bonds. Certainly no stock, other than a few shares of Lebenthal & Company, Inc. (until Mother died in 1994, and I came into her shares). And aside from a small amount of MBIA stock that I bought as a show of faith in a public company where I was a director, I owned no other stocks. I wasn't interested in equities, and I had no money to play with, anyway. But when money dropped into my lap after the sale of the firm, I became, not only a planner of my own finances, but a prospect for every financial instrument that I had either sold or ever railed against. When it came to investing my own money, what would I do? Would I take my own advice? Would I practice what I preached?

About Munis. Here's What I Told the Client. What I Did for Myself. Compare Them.

What I Told the Client: *If you're sure you'll need your money in the foreseeable future, you should invest in bonds that mature accordingly. You can always sell your bonds before maturity. But why subject your savings to the vagaries of the market? If you have no timetable for the reuse of your money, but just might need it some time in the distant future, stagger your maturities. Build a ladder. (That's the name for a portfolio that is scheduled to return your investment at regular intervals, so you're never all short, never all long, never all wrong.)*—Lebenthal Newsletter, *July 26, 2002.*

What I Did for Myself: With half the money I invested in munis, I took my own advice. I *did* stagger that first half, putting equal amounts in one- to six-year bonds, so I would have money coming in right along—one, two, three, four, five, six years out. The other half went into the longest maturities I could lay my hands on (for their higher interest and superior cash flow now, not in the year 2020, but right now). Splitting it 50-50 between a bunch of short bonds and a bunch of long bonds is known as a "Barbell Strategy." But *laddering* those one- to six-year maturities at the "short end" of my barbell—while skipping the rungs in between—and going for the best return I could nail down at the long end, is what I call the "Lebenthal Modified Barbell Portfolio." Why skip the middle years? Listen, at my age I saw no sense in staggering maturities much beyond six years, certainly not all the way out to 2030. If my intention was to reinvest as bonds mature, I'd have to wait until I was over 100 for all the bonds in my ladder to mature and be entirely replaced by new ones. Oh, another thing you should know. Bond calls before maturity can screw up a carefully planned ladder. So for the purposes of laddering, I think of a 20-year bond with a 10-year call as a 10-year bond, a 10-year bond with a 5-year call as a 5-year bond, and so forth.

I always think of bond calls as ants at a picnic. I had to learn about ants at picnics the hard way, for my very first client Sol Dobin. Way back in the early 1960s, I sold Sol a NYC Housing Authority 3 percent bond of 2001. At a premium, mind you! Who ever thought a 3 percent bond would be called? Who? The Housing Authority, that's who. And only a few short months after the trade, they called the bonds. Sol's yield to the call? Don't ask. But you asked, so I'll tell you: negative 2 percent, because Sol paid a premium and got back only par.

To make amends, I took Sol to lunch at Delmonico's and ran up a tab on a couple of filet mignons that at least reduced his net loss to zero. Or would have, if I hadn't forgotten my wallet, and Sol had to pick up the tab. What else could I say to Sol but a generous, "Sorry old sport, screwed again!"

(Today, the Municipal Securities Rule Making Board requires quoting premium bonds that are callable at "yield-to-call" or "yield-to-maturity," whichever is worse. Calls are part of the game. And rest assured if a bond is callable and it behooves the issuer to call in a high coupon bond and bump the bondholder out of the picture, he will.)

What I Told the Client: *Let's say you want income to live on now. Go for bonds with the highest "coupon" or interest rates. If you have to pay a premium, pay it. After all, the premium is part of the investment and earns the same interest as every other penny of the investment (just as $1,001 in the bank earns interest on the $1 as well as on the $1,000).—From Lebenthal's* Municipal Bond Information Kit.

What I Did for Myself: Who would ever pay 115 for a bond knowing in five years they would get back only 100? Who? Me! (Who else?) I bought bonds with a 7.10 percent coupon, meaning I would be getting $71 a year triple tax-free in New York City for every $1,150 I put in now. By my back-of-the-envelope arithmetic, only $40 of that would be "new" money. The other $30 would be my own money, the premium coming back to me every six months in the coupon as return of capital. I was only earning a true yield to maturity of 3.75 percent. But that didn't matter to me. I didn't mind getting my own money back. Because my deal with the new company that owned us almost dictated that I had to dip into capital to live. As far as I was concerned, the premium coming back to me bit by bit every time I got my interest could be considered what mother used to call, "an orderly invasion of capital." And invade capital I must.

What I Told the Client: *TSASC stands for Tobacco Settlement Asset Securitization Corporation. Those bonds are for the infrastructure and capital improvements that make New York City work. The money to pay interest and principal comes from the pockets of the cigarette companies for every cigarette sold, in settlement of the various lawsuits by the States against the tobacco companies. The Master Settlement Agreement settled only the health care claims of the states. It does not release the manufacturers who settled, from liability in individual, class action, or federal government claims. What if all those claims and outstanding judgments bankrupt the tobacco companies? What about competition from discounters, bootleggers, and companies that are not part of the Master Settlement Agreement? What if people stop smoking? Not only Moody's, Standard & Poor's, and Fitch, but the bond market itself rates the bonds. And when bonds of comparable maturity and rating are paying less than 5 percent and TSASCs are paying more than 7 percent, price is telling you something: Friends don't let friends buy too many Tobacco Bonds. For me more than 10 percent of a portfolio constitutes undue concentration.*—Lebenthal Newsletters, *August 8, 2002 and May 7, 2004.*

What I Did for Myself: I put 5 percent of my muni-bond portfolio into TSASCs. I also put 5 percent of my munibond portfolio into New York State Dormitory Authority Bonds for the Mount Sinai/New York University Health Obligated Group, which are rated below investment grade. A total of 10 percent of my portfolio is bonds that would curl the Founding Mother's hair. But at least, I put my money where my mouth was, and not one penny more.

What I Told the Client: *Here is some advice from the "Life Is To Live" Department: The time to invest is when you have the funds. You'll hit some markets. You'll miss some. But this is not a business of getting in at the bottom and out at the top. If municipal bonds are a better buy for you in your own particular tax bracket than the taxable alternatives, then the right time to invest is when you have the funds.—From innumerable conversations on the telephone with Lebenthal clients.*

What I Did for Myself: As we go to press, I am sitting with 10 percent of my money in what [on my monthly statement] is called "Cash and Cash Equivalents." This money is invested in a very short tax-exempt instrument that rolls my money over every seven days and then renews it for another seven days, at whatever the going rate for seven-day paper happens to be—which right now is only a few pennies more than I'd get leaving my money in a mattress. But I'm not hungry for the yield on this money. I'm looking for liquidity. Do I really need the cash? No. Do I think I will? No. Then why am I doing it? Because I'm human, just like those holdout clients of mine who tell me they don't like long-term interest rates and are waiting for interest rates to go up. I'm admitting it: I'm keeping my options open with 10 percent of my money. Even after four years. I am still *Waiting for Godot.* Do I have any reason to think interest rates will go up? Up high enough to bring inflation and the yields of yesteryear back from the dead and make the cost of waiting worthwhile? Sure I do, if any of these cataclysms come to pass:

Foreign savings that now finance America's consumption binge and deficits would have to disappear.

Man—the unstoppable builder of the pyramids, cathedrals, dikes, and canals—would have to take on the building of a mighty (and inflationary) seawall against the rising tides of warming oceans in this brave, new post-Katrina world.

The democracies would have to finance a modern-day crusade to bring the Great Society to the Eastern world.

And, at home, government would have to eat the burgeoning health care cost of a population, half of whom, born today, will live to a hundred.

The price of oil would have to surpass $70 . . . $80 . . . or whatever it takes to exceed the contribution to productivity that could possibly come from a barrel of oil.

Government borrowing for everyday expenses (with nothing to show for the money), and the exponential burden of paying interest on interest, would have to continue unabated.

Europeans, pulling together, growing their economies, having to raise their interest rates, would have to give our interest rates a real run for the money.

You ask me, "Do I think any of these things could happen?" I've got to say, "Yes, they could if life and death causes and the survival of the human race suddenly took precedence over mere money."

Bonds versus Stocks

What I Told the Client: *During the not-so-hot mood swing of the stock market in the mid seventies, the young men in the mod suits and $50 haircuts who were selling stocks (and are now driving cabs), used to fall back on a statistic from the University of Chicago Business School study. The mantra was that if you bought one of every share traded on the Exchange since 1925, and held through thick and thin, ups and downs, splits and reinvested dividends, you would have made over 9 percent a year, before taxes. That is, if you had bought one of every share. If you had held. If you had survived the Depression, the subsequent bear markets, the short-term risks that go into the life and death process. The trouble is that nobody buys averages. You buy this or you buy that. So, the sum of J. Paul Getty's success and yours and a million other people's successes (or disappointments) over a 40-year period, may add up to a statistical gain of 9 percent. But*

swell consolation that is, if you're one of the losers. It re-
minds me of what the surgeon said to the fellow on the
table when he asked what his chances were. "One hun-
dred percent if you make it. Zero if you don't."—Lebenthal Newsletter, *February 1, 1974.*

What I Did for Myself: I bought stocks. I bought them
for me personally. And I bought them for a trust for my
kids. And I didn't choose them on my own. I left the stock
picking to my portfolio manager at an outside equity management firm. He didn't buy the Dow or the S&P 500 or the
Russell 2000. He didn't buy the "stock market" or any particular style, slice, or sliver of it. He bought businesses. He
doesn't believe in "momentum," or "growth" or "technical
analysis." He believes in *businesses,* and after judging the
intrinsic value of a company, he pays less than he thinks
that company is worth. Now, who is this wunderkind to
whom I, the shiner of my own shoes, the writer of my own
TV spots, the maker of my own bed, have given such un-
characteristic freedom with my dough? None other than
my son Jimmy Lebenthal, the U.S. Navy trained nuclear
submariner, the Goldman Sachs trained investment advi-
sor, now turned portfolio manager at Levy, Harkins &
Company, Inc.

Eating My Words

I cannot believe what I said to Senators Al D'Amato of New
York and Ted Stevens of Alaska—in front of witnesses yet—
about painting assholes out of chipmunks at Disney before

ever, ever selling a *taxable* municipal bond. But that was before I discovered "risk management" and "Modern Portfolio Theory," becoming a devotee of "asset allocation," and buying them for myself. Taxable munis were a spawn of the 1986 Tax Reform Act, for local necessities Congress deemed "nongovernmental" and so unworthy of federal tax exemption.

What I Told the Client: *The goal of risk management is to increase return without commensurately increasing risk and, conversely, to reduce risk without commensurately reducing return. How do you do this and not just have risk and reward cancel each other out? You do it:*

- *By diversifying among truly diversifiable asset classes that move independently of each other.*
- *By looking at each security for its contribution to overall portfolio risk.*
- *By adjusting your expectations for return, up or down, to how wide of the mark returns have been historically.*
- *By being realistic about expecting to get 16 percent out of an investment just because it has averaged 16 percent, when that 16 percent reflects years that were above 16 percent and years below.*
- *By forgetting this business of trying to "beat the market," and accepting the basic tenet of Modern Portfolio Theory. What you buy (asset allocation) is more important than when you buy (market timing).*—Lebenthal Newsletter, *April 1, 2005.*

What I Did for Myself: Talk about diversifying—I now sell to clients both tax-free and taxable munis. I sell corporate bonds, federal agencies, mutual funds, common and preferred shares of leveraged closed end bond funds. And with my own money, I have become a walking asset allocation pie chart.

I own munis, equities, money market instruments, and a Real Estate Investment Trust. (What's in your REIT? Real estate? The actual properties? Mine has mortgage-backed securities that are issued by agencies of the United States government.) And I just did an unheard-of thing for someone my age. I bought an Immediate Pay Annuity with the money in my 401(k) (that otherwise would be subject to a 55 percent hit in estate taxes). But I didn't do it just for tax reasons. I did it for the same reason I buy high coupon munis at enormous premiums: "Orderly Invasion of Capital." I need the income from the annuity for Jackie's care and maintenance for the rest of her life, with the kids getting back any unused principal.

In a show of ecumenical largesse, I wrote the equivalent (for readability and friendliness) of another Lebenthal bond kit on CMOs with all the graphs done in child-like Crayola crayons, unlike the productions of venerable mortgage-bankers. I put the stock that I received from the sale of Lebenthal into a Goldman Sachs Exchange Fund and took back shares in a diversified pool of other companies. I recently engaged in some fancy footwork and "sold a covered call" on the MBIA stock I received in deferred compensation for 16 years on the Board. And, yes, I played the currency market, invested in an oil pipeline. And I have cash parked in a long-term bond that's very liquid. This paradox is explained by its variable coupon rate. The interest I get every week floats instead of the bond itself, which means resale value is kept at or near par.

In keeping with my "Second Law of Modern Portfolio Theory " (that means looking at each security for its contribution to overall portfolio risk and not just at its own riskiness), I am willing to weigh the pros and cons of *any* investment opportunity—not just for its own volatility—but for its ability to offset ups and down in the rest of the portfolio. But I'm from the Warren Buffett school of humility that says, "If you can't explain an investment opportunity to your spouse, that's God's way of telling you to avoid it." And I'll go Buffett one further: Your spouse (or, reasonably intelligent loved one) must be able to explain the investment to you. Let's see if "interest rate swaps" pass the test, as described here by my son-in-law, Jeremy Diamond.

Let's say a savings and loan (S&L) has extended a 15-year fixed-rate mortgage of 4.0 percent, with cash from its depositors. Let's say the S&L pays its depositors a rate of LIBOR (London Interbank Offered Rate) plus 1 percent. And let's say LIBOR, a floating rate at which banks are borrowing from other banks, is currently 1.5 percent. So right now the S&L is paying depositors 2.5 percent and making a spread of 1.5 percent (4 percent minus 2.5 percent equals 1.5 percent).

In the event rates rose and the S&L had to pay more on its deposits, its spread will be compressed, or even turn negative (if LIBOR plus 1 percent should exceed 4 percent). To protect against this outcome, the treasurer of the S&L would enter into a swap with a counterparty in which he agrees to pay the counterparty an amount of 4 percent (equal

208

to the cash flow from the mortgage) and receive in exchange a floating rate of LIBOR plus 2 percent.

Don't forget, the S&L, will still be paying its depositors LIBOR plus 1 percent, while now receiving LIBOR plus 2 percent from the swap counterparty. So, no matter what happens to that floating LIBOR rate, the S&L has locked in a steady 1 percent by essentially turning its floating rate interest liability into a fixed one. (Fixed in the sense that LIBOR plus 2 will always beats LIBOR plus 1 by a fixed 1 percent.) Now the S&L can continue in the business of making more mortgage loans without fear of ever rising interest rates wiping out all its profits on older mortgage loans.

Thank you, Jay, but I'm just enough of a curmudgeon to cut a wide swath to avoid a trade in one thing that can go up and down and whose performance depends on a trade in a second thing that can go up and down. So that when neither pans out like long-term capital and the hedge fund recently with the play on the stock of GM and the bonds of GM, you sink in the morass both ways. Let's just say, "Interest rate swaps? Put me down as doubtful."

It Isn't Stocks or Bonds. It's Both.

What I Told the Client: *You buy Municipal Bonds for income. Super income because it's tax free. You do not buy them to speculate. The place to speculate, is in the stock market, gold, real estate, Tiffany Lamps, and Fiesta Ware. Not in bonds. Entirely too much time is being spent in the bond market these days bottom watching. Bullish? Bearish? Neither has anything to do with the bond market. We re-peat. You buy municipal bonds for income. Not to buy and sell because you think you are going to make money from market moves.*—Lebenthal Newsletter, *December 31, 1981.*

What I Did for Myself: After living all those years with the one arrow in my quiver (municipal bonds) and the one string on my fiddle (municipal bonds), I learned, and I grew. I wish I hadn't disparaged investing in stocks as speculating, putting equities in the same boat with the collectible dishes theater owners handed out free to moviegoers in the Great Depression that are now going for hundreds of dollars a set. Because, these days, it is not stocks or bonds. It is both. Studies of risk versus return for stocks and bonds from 1970 to 1997 by Ibbotson Associates showed that a portfolio of 25 percent stocks, 75 percent bonds would have produced about 10 percent more overall portfolio return and approximately 5 percent less risk than a portfolio of 100 percent bonds over that 27-year period.

I'm convinced that somewhere between a portfolio of 100 percent bonds and 100 percent stocks would be the "optimum portfolio." That means you can't shoot for any more yield without increasing your risk. And you can't eliminate any more risk without reducing your return. So it is not just bonds for income and stocks for growth. It is the symbiotic combination of the two, managing the risk (and reward) of the whole portfolio.

So how am I doing? I just got a report from son Jimmy. I'm down $^{52}/_{100}$s of 1 percent in my equity portfolio for the quarter. But I didn't invest for the quarter. I invested for the "long haul." Ask me in a few years, and if I'm still down, I will tell you. I didn't invest for a few years. I invested for the long haul. Modern Portfolio Theory is a theory, which means you gotta believe. I'm a spry and optimistic 77. Investing for the long haul requires attitude: It is not only me, it is my money that counts. And if you don't believe that your money has a life of its own, just ask your heirs.

LEBENTHAL TO GO

Savings refer to money you can
put your hands on in a pinch.
Investing means savings you can
afford not to touch. Speculating is,
well, I wouldn't know.
I don't have any play money.

Having an opinion gives the
salesman authority. Having
money gives the client even more.

If you cannot understand an
investment, be grateful. It's
God's way of telling you to avoid it.

13

Go, Girl!

Oh, dark, unasked-for day! On December 2, 2005, a
full 80 years after Mother and Dad hung out their
shingle and proudly announced the birth of
"Lebenthal & Co., for the transaction of a general investment bond business, specializing in municipal bonds,"
Lebenthal, An AXA Financial Business, Division of Advest,
Inc., ceased to exist.

Back on December 3, 2001, Alexandra and I had sold
Lebenthal for $25 million to Advest, Inc. Advest was a sprawl-
ing conglomeration of entrepreneurial brokers and financial
advisors spread around the country with no particular all-for-
one, one-for-all identity. For us, the money meant less than
the opportunity to expand Lebenthal overnight into a national brand. Just as when French Fragrances International
bought Elizabeth Arden and changed its name to Arden, Advest would bring its 500 or so brokers and far-flung branches
together under the umbrella of the Lebenthal name.

For four years the strategy inched along. Advest opened
or changed the name of six branches to Lebenthal. And 40

new brokers could be called Lebenthal Heroes. But then, with no more say than Alexandra and I would have over the Big Bang and the expanding and shrinking of stars in the galaxy, AXA decided it wanted to exit the securities business. Merrill Lynch wanted to expand and ka-jing! AXA sold Advest to Merrill Lynch. In the deal, Lebenthal was simply a jewel thrown in with the crown.

My first reaction was typically me: "Hey, this could be good!" I quickly envisioned the proliferation of the Lebenthal name through Merrill Lynch's mighty organization. My euphoria lasted until Merrill Lynch held a broker's briefing in our office and I heard the innocent-sounding phrase "Merrill Lynch Architecture." I knew instantly that the blithe, intuitive, highly personalized Lebenthal spirit, personified by the Lebenthal Newsletter, Lebenthal advertising, Lebenthal bond kit, Lebenthal name, and by the Lebenthals themselves, Alexandra and me, would never fit in a company that describes its way of dealing with people as "architecture."

In the meantime, Alexandra tried to get Merrill Lynch to sell us back the family business so that we could maintain the Lebenthal brand as a shining landmark on New York City's business skyline. Merrill Lynch listened politely but was unmoved.

My response was identical to how I have faced over 40 years of other crises in the municipal bond business:

Like the Fiscal Collapse of New York City.

Like the Social Security tax on municipal bonds.

Like the 1986 Tax Reform Act.

Like the early call of those New York City Housing Development Corporation 12¾s.

I would run a full-page ad in the *New York Times.* Make it a half page. On second thought, maybe a quarter page would do. Anyway, in all its glory, here is the ad I never ran:

Dear Merrill Lynch,
Please use my name because...

When you aquired Lebenthal's parent company, Advest, Inc., a jewel got thrown in with the crown: a priceless treasure, rarer and even more precious than our bodies and our assets. I'm talking about the Lebenthal Brand.

All by itself, the name Lebenthal conjures up the idea of looking after people, treating them like family, being our brother's keeper, giving investors the information they need to decide "Yes..." or "No."

It is no accident that my last name has turned municipal bonds into household words. Bright, straight-talking advertising has seared Lebenthal into the consciousness of the greatest city in the world. But striving to live up to the advertising has made the name a pleasure to do business with.

I can't tell you the kick I get, when I call a client and can hear a husband or wife calling out to a spouse, "Honey, its Lebenthal!"

When Merrill Lynch briefed us on our new home-to-be, I thought to myself, "Could be good." Then I learned, bit by bit, that Lebenthal advertising and newsletters, name and identity, would gradually cease to exist.

It's not me I'm worried about. I'm worried about the loss of a shining landmark in the municipal bond market and, for that matter, on the whole business skyline of New York City. That's why letting the name Lebenthal wither on the vine would be a little like tearing down a Penn Station, again.

So, if you have no plans to use the name Lebenthal, Alexandra and I will make you a business offer that's worth your while to sell us back our name.

LEBENTHAL

I never ran the ad because I wasn't all that sure Merrill Lynch indeed had no use for the Lebenthal name and brand, nor, for that matter, Alexandra or me. Then Robert J. McCann, vice chairman at Merrill Lynch, was quoted in the *New York Times*, saying Merrill would not use the Lebenthal name in any corporate capacity. He did say that if the Lebenthal brokers being acquired by Merrill Lynch, "feel it is advantageous to use Lebenthal in how they market their individual teams, then that is an option we will allow," adding the coup de grace, "I wish Alexandra and her father nothing but success."

Let me tell you a little something about my daughter. When Alexandra took the reins on July 4, 1995, as the third generation of Lebenthals to head Lebenthal, that ended any unprofessional "daddykins" and "babykins" in the Lebenthal & Company corridors of power. I had passed the torch for real. And I insisted that Alexandra replace me on radio and television as the company's spokeswoman. If I got hit by a truck, I didn't want the market to say "Uh oh! There goes Lebenthal."

Not to sound like that sourpuss Antonio Salieri in the movie *Amadeus* when the Mozart kid grabs the ball and runs with it, some thanks I got from Alexandra for the perks of celebrity I handed over to her. She promptly bumped me right out of the spotlight and became the industry's bond expert on the cable television business shows and, of course, on Lou Rukeyser's *Wall Street Week*. She absolutely ran the business of the Lebenthal business. She took over the municipal bond department of Advest. And overnight she became a star.

At the same time, Alexandra did tell me to, "stick around." I suspect that while she fully intended to put her own stamp on the advertising, she wanted to retain a little of the old man's touch.

And that's what I did as Lebenthal's Chairman Emeritus: I continued writing the newsletters and the copy for Alexandra's commercials, and from 9 to 5 played philosopher king for the House of Lebenthal.

The next chapter for the House that Louis and Sayra Lebenthal, Eleanor and Gerry Bissinger, Jim and Alexandra Lebenthal built, is being written as we go to press. Alexandra and I will start anew.

As Alexandra confided to 1,000 admiring fans at a United Jewish Appeal Federation dinner where she was the Wall Street Young Leadership honoree, "I stand before you as Alexandra Lebenthal—not with the actual family business behind me—but as the Alexandra Lebenthal who will be forever grateful for the benefits, advantages, and values of that family business which are now a part of me . . . as I continue on an even greater journey.

Go, girl! Daddykins is behind you.

LEBENTHAL TO GO

Your parents gave you your name.
It's yours to do what you want with.
Your public's goodwill
turned it into a brand.
How's that for a debt to society?

Index

M

Shackelton, Laura, 1–2
Showmanship, 2–3
"Sibling Wars," 20
Simon, Treasury Secretary
    Bill, 58–59
Social Security tax, on
    munis, 87, 98–99
Soros, George, 89
South Carolina v. Baker, 99
Stapp, Colonel John Paul,
    176
Stern, Dr. Aaron, 21–22
Stevens, Senator Ted, 205
Stocks, adding to bond
    portfolio, 45–46,
    209–211
Sullivan, Annie, 174

T

Tagliani, John, 89
"Talking Surgeon," the,
    36–37
Tax exemption, history of,
    97–101
Tax Reform Act of 1986,
    97–98
Tenth Amendment, 99
This I Believe, 69

Time and timing, 28–32,
    81–82
T Is for Tumbleweed, 4
Tobacco Settlement Asset
    Securitization
    Corporation, 201
Tough Hombre, 30–32

U

U.S. Conference of Mayors
    speech, 158–166

V

Volatility, 88–91
"Verities," 16–17
Volcker, Paul, 33

W

Wachner, Linda, 132
Wainwright, Loudon, 85–86
"Wall Street Week," 40
Washington, George, 43
Washington Public Power
    Supply System, 93–96